Stretch, Bend & Boggle

A week-by-week
maths program for developing logic
and problem-solving skills

Brian Stokes

Second edition

Illustrations by Carolyn Smith & Michael Burnett

HAWKER BROWNLOW
E D U C A T I O N

Cover Designer: Eva Ming Ling Kam
Book Designers: Eva Ming Ling Kam & Susana Siew-Demunck

Published in Australia by
HAWKER BROWNLOW
E D U C A T I O N

First edition published in 1993 by Toha Kape Ltd
Second edition © 2004 Hawker Brownlow Education
P.O. Box 580, Moorabbin,
Victoria 3189, Australia
Phone: (03) 9555 1344 Fax: (03) 9553 4538
Toll Free Ph: 1800 33 4603 Fax: 1800 15 0445
Website: http://www.hbe.com.au
Email: orders@hbe.com.au

All rights reserved
Printed in Australia

National Library of Australia Cataloguing-in-Publication entry:

Stokes, Brian.
Stretch, bend and boggle.

ISBN 1 74101 244 9.

1. Mathematical recreations. 2. Games in mathematics
education. 3. Homework. I. Title.

372.72044

Code: HB2449
1204

Contents

Acknowledgements

Few problem setters can claim to be original. This series has 'something old, something new, something borrowed, something blue'. I have borrowed freely ideas from puzzlers going back more than a century and tried to vary and update them to interest today's generation.

Some authors have been so prolific and original that it would be churlish not to acknowledge my debt. Lewis Carroll, Henry Ernest Dudeney, Hubert Phillips, Sam Loyd, J.A.H Hunter, Williams and Savage, R.M. Lucey, Isaac Asimov, D. St. P. Barnard, Martin Gardner, Eric Emmet, Boris Kordemsky and Raymond Smullyan are among those who have given wry pleasure to millions over the years.

Closer to home, this book could not have been written without the critical support of Bruce Love who worked through the problems, trialling many of them with students; Philip Stokes who provided initial sketches; Carolyn Smith who illustrated the book; and the staff of the Waikato Education Centre who helped prepare it for publication; however, I claim total ownership of any faults and would appreciate their being brought to my attention.

I am also most grateful to my wife, Kathy, and my family for their encouragement and for putting up with a rather annoying single-mindedness over several months.

Note to the second edition: A new section called 'Holiday Stretch' has been added to this edition, with a set of questions to be attempted in each vacation. An index of titles in the Benders and Bogglers sections has been added to facilitate reference.

For this second edition my thanks go to Barbara Hudson of the Hamilton Education Resource Centre for her continuing encouragement; to Elaine Brownlow and the staff at Hawker Brownlow Education; and to Michael Burnett for his illustrations for the Holiday Stretch section.

Brian Stokes

Introduction

Stretch, Bend and Boggle is a book of logical and mathematical problems for all those who relish stimulation and challenge. It is particularly suitable for students at secondary school who have some experience in problem-solving techniques and cooperative-learning approaches, have a sound knowledge of basic numeration, and want something better than a monotonous diet of techniques and examples divorced from the real world.

The aim throughout is to provide material to develop process skills in mathematics, such as thinking, selecting strategies, teamwork, checking and reflecting.

Almost all of the problems can be solved by the mathematics studied by Year 7. None requires mathematical knowledge beyond a normal Year 10 syllabus.

Rationale

When there is too heavy an emphasis on methods in mathematics, its inherently logical nature is often ignored; research has consistently shown that children's logical abilities are usually of a high order compared with their actual achievements in primary mathematics. Students have commonly reported on their wish for the stimulating challenges this book offers.

Thomas Edison truly said 'Genius is one per cent inspiration and ninety-nine per cent perspiration', and it is regrettably true in this age of instant everything that perseverance does not get its due credit. With most of these problems, there is no instant fix, and some sustained thought is required; 'If at first you don't succeed, try, try again.'

Ever since George Polya wrote his book *How to Solve It* [1], it has been increasingly realised that a few basic strategies are invaluable when trying to unravel a knotty problem. Most teachers and many students will by now be very familiar with some of these strategies, which include:

- guess and check
- work systematically
- use reasoning
- look for a pattern

- solve a simpler problem
- draw a diagram
- make a chart or table
- make a model
- act it out
- work backwards
- write down an equation
- compare with a similar problem.

Suggested strategies for the Stretchers problems are included in the answers.

A laudable development in mathematics education is the acknowledgement of the value of working together and discussion for problems with no obvious line of approach. Most of the problems in the book lend themselves to such cooperative activity. One aim has been to enable the problem to be posed in a very brief time; teachers may embellish if they wish.

Structure of the book

Stretchers are designed to be quickly stated, to have relatively straightforward answers and often to allow further investigation. In each set there is a mixture of problem types. For a class it is intended that problems should not take much more than ten minutes, including discussion time. They are particularly suitable as general motivators and warming-up exercises. The answers given are intended to be concise.

Benders will take longer and are very suitable for problem-solving by a group; in each of the ten sets there are problems on logic, algebra, geometry and number, and there is an alphametic. There is a hint for each problem as well as full answers and commentary.

Bogglers are longer and often harder even though they require no more mathematical knowledge. Again there is a hint for each question, and full answers with explanations are provided.

For those who are unsure how to go about solving logical problems, there are notes after the answers to Week 1, Problem 2 and Week 2, Problem 3; hints on how to solve alphametics are given in the note after Week 1, Problem 5.

The format is designed to lend itself to a variety of organisational patterns. If the Stretchers are used daily, there are more than enough for a school year; alternatively, they can be used to introduce a topic, to provide variety, to extend fast workers or to conclude a block of work. Alternative uses for Benders and Bogglers are as 'Problem of the week', as an ongoing project problem or for a mathematics competition. Teachers who wish to group Benders and Bogglers according to technique will find a summary in the Appendix.

References

[1] G. Polya *How to Solve It. A New Aspect of Mathematical Method* (Princeton University Press 1971 2nd edition).

Stretchers

Stretchers are designed to be quickly stated, to have relatively straightforward answers, and often to allow further investigation. In each set there is a mixture of problem types. For a class it is intended that problems should not take much more than 10 minutes including discussion time. They are particularly suitable as general motivators and warming-up exercises. The answers given are intended to be concise.

Stretchers

Stretchers are designed to be quickly stated, to have relatively straightforward answers, and often to allow further investigation. In each set there is a mixture of problem types. For a class it is intended that problems should not take much more than 10 minutes including discussion time. They are particularly suitable as general motivators and warming-up exercises. The answers given are intended to be concise.

Note: Problems marked * may require unfamiliar material or may be difficult.

Week 1

1. A knockout competition attracts 75 entries, and a bye is used every time an odd number is left for a round. How many matches are played?

2. Betty sat at a square table with drivers of a bus, a van and a truck. She sat on Tania's left and Pat sat on the van driver's right. If Alison (who sat opposite Tania) is not the truck driver, who drives the bus?

3. 'Aba, Baba and Caba are joined by three straight roads. It is 3 km from Aba to Caba, 8 km from Baba to Aba and 4 km from Caba to Baba.' What is wrong with this statement?

4. Four mirrors form a rectangle 3 m by 2 m. A light beam is shone from *A* at 45 degrees. Which corner does the beam strike first?

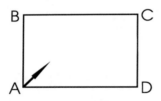

5. 3 × NEW = WINE. What digits do the letters represent?

Week 2

1.   What day was 1 January 2004?

2.   If AA × A = BB and AA + A = AC, what different digits do A, B and C stand for?

3.   On the island of Koo there are two tribes, the Goodies who always tell the truth and the Fixers who always lie. You meet three people. If A says 'All of us are Fixers' and B says 'Just one of us is a Goodie', to which tribe do A, B and C belong?

4.   How can you cut a cube with one straight cut to obtain an equilateral triangle?

5.   If my three children have ages which add to 21 and multiply to 75, how old are they?

Week 3

1. What is the smallest number of triangles needed to make up a regular decagon?

2. The number of eggs in a magic basket doubles each minute. If the basket was full after one hour, when was it half full?

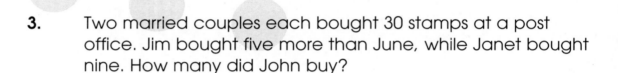

3. Two married couples each bought 30 stamps at a post office. Jim bought five more than June, while Janet bought nine. How many did John buy?

4. Polly knew all the members of her gym, a third by their name and face, and half by their face only. If she knew five only by name, how many were in the club?

5. Two squares are removed from a rectangle, leaving a smaller rectangle 2 cm by 3 cm. What is the largest possible size of the original rectangle?

Week 4

1.   Put in three straight fences to isolate each tree.

2.   A fish weighs 6 kg plus a third of its own weight. How heavy is it?

3.   Two pairs of distinct positive whole numbers are such that the sum of their products is 11 and the product of their sums is 30. Find the pairs.

4.   On the Island of Koo (where Goodies tell the truth and Fixers lie) D says 'I am a Fixer and E is a Goodie.' What are D and E?

5.   Malcolm has two independent fuel-saving inventions; one saves 30% and the other 20%. What percentage do they save when used together?

Week 5

1. Find, without a calculator, the remainder when 4444 is divided by 18.

2. Six glasses are arranged in a row so that the first three glasses are full and the last three empty. How can you move just one glass to make the row of glasses alternately full and empty?

3. A cube is painted then cut up into 27 smaller cubes. How many of these are painted on just two sides?

4. How many squares are there with a dot at each corner?

● ● ●
● ● ●
● ● ●

5. How many differently shaped triangles can be made, using six unbroken matchsticks each time?

Week 6

1. Peter and Marilyn are using rods placed end-to-end to make trains. Peter has ten 7-cm rods and Marilyn has ten 9-cm rods. Peter's train was 1 cm shorter than Marilyn's. How many rods did each use?

2. Two engines each pulling two carriages have to pass on a single-line railway. If one engine and one carriage can fit on the siding, how do the trains pass?

3. If EEL + EEL = LEAP, find PLEA.

4. The Fusiliers march at 120 paces to the minute, while the Rifles march at 180 paces to the minute. If both regiments start marching together (right feet down), when will their left feet first be down together?

    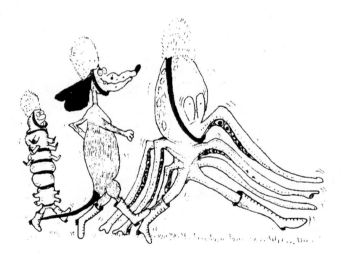

5. An oblong whose dimensions are an exact number of centimetres has the same area in square centimetres as its perimeter in centimetres. What are its dimensions?

Week 7

1. If two numbers are both positive, why is the square of their sum always greater than the sum of their squares?

2. Last year the bills for club subscriptions (an exact number of dollars between $2 and $20) requested in addition a $1 donation towards a club outing. If all the members except one gave the donation with their subscription and the total receipts were $300, how many members were there?

3. The hands of a clock are together at midday. When are they next together?

4. How many 10-cent coins can you lay around another 10-cent coin on a level surface so that they all touch it?

5. In a survey it was found that 77% of respondents drank coffee, 71% drank tea and 48% drank both. How many drank neither tea nor coffee?

Week 8

1. A square swimming pool has a tree at each corner. How can you double the area of the pool and keep it square without removing the trees?

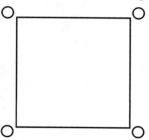

2. What are the prime factors of 111?

3. In how many ways can the faces of a tetrahedron be coloured if each face is to be either red or green?

4. In an indoor sports club of 40 members, 30 play darts, 30 play snooker and 30 play dominoes. At least how many must play all three?

5. A circle is divided into five equal sectors with each sector orange, blue or green. How many different patterns (excluding rotations) are there if adjacent sectors are coloured differently?

Week 9

1. In how many ways can you arrange the letters of the word GROUP?

2. A knockout competition attracts 75 entries and a preliminary round is held so that there will be no byes later. How many entries must play in that round?

3. My collection of spiders and beetles has 8 heads and 54 legs. How many are there of each?

4. Alec said 'It was Charlie'; Beth said 'No it wasn't'; Charlie said ' It was Alec'. If only the offender lied, whodunit?

5. How many regular hexagons are there in this figure?

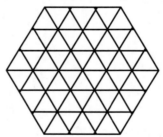

Week 10

1. Six girls were standing in a circle. Every alternate girl had blue eyes and every third girl had fair hair. How many had neither?

2. A camera and its case cost $110. If the camera costs $100 more than the case, what is the cost of the case?

3. In how many ways can the faces of a tetrahedron be coloured if each face is to be red, yellow or blue and all colours are used?

4. On the island of Koo (where the Goodies tell the truth and the Fixers lie) H says 'J is a _____', but the word was lost in the sound of the surf. H and J were of different tribes. Did H say 'Goodie' or 'Fixer'?

5. A 2-litre bottle is in the form of a cylinder which narrows near the top. An ingenious way to find the volume of liquid when partly filled is to measure from the base to the level of liquid with the bottle upright, then inverted. If the distances are 5 cm and 3 cm respectively, how much liquid is there?

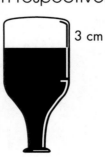

5 cm

3 cm

Week 11

1. I think of a number, double it, add one, square the result and add nine. What is the least possible answer?

2. The club outing had been a disaster. The following year subscriptions were raised (though still an exact number of dollars less than $20) and a $1 donation requested. Only one member gave the donation but $300 was received. How many members paid their subscriptions?

3. Every time Troll crossed the bridge his money doubled, but he had to pay a Troll toll of $4 at the end. He thought that was a real money-spinner, but the third toll took all his remaining money. How much did Troll have to start with?

4. A string is wrapped twice around a cylinder of circumference 60 cm to join A and B. If AB is 50 cm, how long is the string?

5. Find the missing number: 1, 5, 17, 53, ____, 485 …

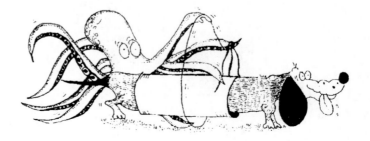

Week 12

1.   A hiker walks up a hill at 3 km/h and down at 6 km/h. What is her average speed?

2.   Find the square roots of 25 × 144 and 25 + 144.

3.   Bradley is a better runner than Mark. He can run three circuits of the track while Mark runs two. If they start together in opposite directions, how many times do they pass before coming together again at the start?

4.   On the island of Koo (where Goodies tell the truth, Fixers lie and the Weasels do both) K says 'I'm a Weasel,' L says 'That's true,' and M says 'I'm not a Weasel.' If there is one of each, what are they?

5.   Can you make seven equilateral triangles using nine matchsticks?

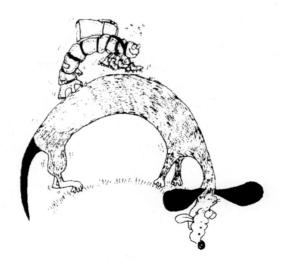

Week 13

1. What is the 31st odd number?

2. A fish at the edge of a circular bowl swam east for 75 cm, reaching the edge of the bowl, then north for 100 cm, once more reaching the edge. What was the diameter of the aquarium?

3. How many different bracelets can be made by stringing together two red beads, two green beads and one blue bead, all otherwise identical?

4. Place the numbers 1 to 9 in this diagram so that each side adds to 23.

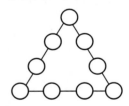

5. Moki asks, 'Can I have a raise, Boss?.' His boss replies, 'There are never more than 366 days in the year; at 8 hours a day that's 122 days. Take away weekends (104 days), annual holidays (14 days) and statutory holidays (at least 4) and you don't even work for me.' Was he being fair?

Week 14

1.   How many corners are there on a cube?

2.   Peter and Sarah had 100 oysters but two of them were bad,
      so they were thrown out. If Peter had eaten four times as
      many as he actually did, Sarah would have eaten only half
      hers. How many did each of them eat?

3.   'Take five pills, one every half hour.' How long will that take?

4.   On the island of Koo (where Goodies tell the truth and Fixers
      always lie) I meet N and P. N says 'At least one of us is a
      Fixer.' What are N and P?

5.   A woman's office and her home are at opposite ends of a
      diameter of a circular railway. If she travels clockwise to
      work it takes her 80 minutes, but if she travels clockwise
      back home it takes her 1 hour and 20 minutes. How come?

Week 15

1. Thirteen flags are evenly spaced from start to finish along a 100-metre track. An athlete running at a constant speed gets to the seventh flag in six seconds. How long did it take altogether for her to reach the finish?

2. A dollar coin is rolled edge to edge around a fixed dollar coin without slipping. How many revolutions has it completed when it gets back to its starting point?

3. King Pompous IV of Boloni detested his father Pompous III, so he banished the numeral 3 from the national counting system (counting 1, 2, 4, 5 …). What is the Bolonian numeral for our 33?

4. CI × V = CCC. The symbols are not Roman. What digits do the letters represent?

5. How many triangles can you make on the grid below with a dot in each corner?

Week 16

1. Each corner number is the sum of the numbers on the two sides which make the corner. Find the side numbers.

    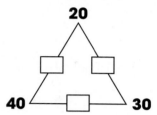

2. How many even primes are there?

3. How many months of the year have 30 days?

4. There are seven 1-dollar coins in a purse. How can you give seven children a dollar each, yet keep a dollar in the purse?

5. Every time Troll crossed the bridge his money doubled, but he had to pay a toll of $2 before crossing. After three crossings Troll was broke. How much did he start with?

Week 17

1. Which two-digit number has a remainder of 2 whether divided by 3, 4, 5 or 6?

2. How many triangles can be formed from five straight lines?

3. I am looking at a picture of a man and say thoughtfully, 'Brothers and sisters have I none, but this man's father is my father's son.' Who is in the picture?

4. Which part of a train is moving in the opposite direction to the rest?

5. Toy cars cost $8 while trucks cost $11. How many of each can be bought for exactly $100?

Week 18

1.   If $(BA)^2 = CCA$ and $A^2 = CA$, what are A, B and C?

2.   How can you cut a cube with one straight cut to get a regular hexagon?

3.   How many triangles are there in this figure?

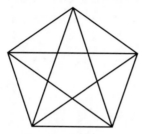

*4.   If three is added to both the numerator and the denominator of a fraction (given in its lowest terms) it doubles in value. What is the fraction?

5.   The price of a book at a sale was reduced by 20%, but the bookseller still had a mark-up of 20%. What was his original mark-up?

Week 19

1. Join all the dots by four connected straight lines.

*2. At what time do both the minute and hour hands of a clock point to an exact minute, with the minute hand four minutes ahead of the hour hand?

3. A train leaves Adelaide for Darwin, travelling at the same speed as another train which left Darwin for Adelaide 2 hours earlier. Which train is nearer Darwin when they meet?

4. What is the next term? 1, 2, 4, 8, 15 …

5. On the island of Koo (where Goodies tell the truth and Fixers lie) S says 'T says I'm a Goodie'. If they come from different tribes, which is which?

Week 20

1. A cube has two faces painted red, two green and two blue. In how many ways can this be done?

2. Maria buys some screws for $1.20. If each screw were 10c cheaper she could buy two more. How many did she buy?

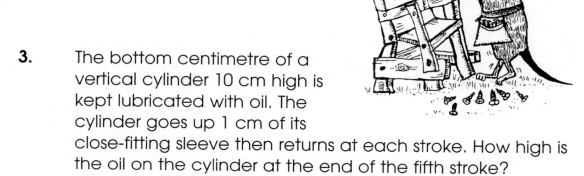

3. The bottom centimetre of a vertical cylinder 10 cm high is kept lubricated with oil. The cylinder goes up 1 cm of its close-fitting sleeve then returns at each stroke. How high is the oil on the cylinder at the end of the fifth stroke?

4. Gibble tells lies only on Sunday, Monday and Tuesday, while Gobble lies only on Wednesday, Thursday and Friday. If A says 'I'm Gibble' and B says 'I'm Gobble', who's who?

5. I have two children who are not both boys. What are the chances that both are girls?

Week 21

1. If a hot tap can fill a bath in 12 minutes, and a cold tap can fill it in 6 minutes, how long does it take to fill the bath with both taps on?

2. Name the only two families of plane quadrilateral which can be constructed using six whole matches.

3. Two of the three children (Alison, Tui and Dan) will eat toast, two will eat cereal and two will eat fruit. One won't eat toast or cereal; Alison won't eat toast or fruit. Who eats what?

4. If $AB^2 = ACC$, what is BA^2?

5. The number on each side of the triangle is the sum of the two numbers at its ends. Find the missing numbers.

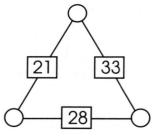

Week 22

1. Five children clubbed together to give their mum a present. Each gave a different whole number of dollars, but no-one gave $2. If the total was $20, how much did each child give?

2. A hotel wants its rooms to be numbered from 1 to 100. How many 9s will be needed?

3. Arrange nine guards symmetrically around a triangular tower so that each side can be seen by exactly five guards.

4. How many diamonds (rhombi) are there?

    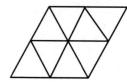

5. A cargo ship leaves Auckland for Sydney, and one leaves Sydney for Auckland each day at the same time. If the trip takes three full days, how many ships from Sydney will one from Auckland pass on the high seas?

Week 23

1. A waterlily doubles its area each day. After 12 days it has a diameter of 2 m. When did it have a diameter of 50 cm?

2. On the island of Koo (where the Goodies tell the truth and the Fixers lie) F said 'I am a Fixer and so is G.' What can you deduce?

3. A party of children lie side by side so that each child has their neighbour's feet next to their head. If five heads are pointing north and five feet are pointing south, how many children must there be?

4. Mrs Bee can fry two steaks at a time in her pan. If a steak takes 30 seconds for each side, what is the least amount of time she needs to fry three steaks?

5. I gave my assistant 20 tomatoes to sell at five for $1 and 40 to sell at five for $2. She sold all 60 at five for $1.50 so I fired her. Why?

Week 24

*1.   My old grandmother's age is a perfect square and equals the difference between the square of my mother's age and the square of my father's age. How old is she?

2.   In how many ways can you get from *A* to *B* along the lines, always approaching *B*?

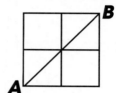

3.   Arrange 18 flower-pots around the sides of a rectangular hall so that there are the same number of pots on each side.

4.   What is the next term? 5, 11, 17, 23, 31 … ?

5.   Ben thinks of a number, doubles it, adds 10, halves the result and takes away the number he first thought of. What is his answer?

Week 25

1. Find two distinct primes whose sum is 14.

2. There are balls of five different colours in a box. How many balls must you pick (sight unseen) to ensure that you have three of the same colour?

3. Show how you can cut a regular tetrahedron to obtain a square.

*4. On the island of Koo (where Goodies tell the truth, Fixers lie and the Weasels are likely to do both), Q says, 'I am more likely to lie than R' and R says, 'That's not true.' What are Q and R?

5. Find out why the sequence: 4, 5, 9, 14, 23, 37... is special by writing the sequences formed by the difference between adjacent terms, and by their sum.

Week 26

1. If Arran is not the youngest then Alice is, and if Alexander is not the youngest, Alice is the oldest. What are their relative ages?

*2. A number with three digits is subtracted from the number with its digits reversed; the difference consists of the same three digits as the original number. What is the number?

3. A blacksmith has to make a single chain from five short chains each of three links. What is the smallest number of links which the blacksmith must open and close?

4. An island 1 metre square is in the middle of a pond 3 metres square. How can you use two 1-metre planks to cross to the island – dry?

5. It is raining at midnight. Will the sun be shining 72 hours later?

Week 27

1. What is the smallest number which has a remainder of 3 when divided by 5, and a remainder of 4 when divided by 6?

2. Find 316 × 25 quickly without a calculator.

3. I have 10 pairs of gloves, all similar, in my drawer. If there are five white pairs and five black pairs, how many gloves must I select to be sure of a pair?

4. Alice, Bill, Cara and Donald are playing bridge. Alice is not opposite Bill who is not to Cara's right. If Cara is not on Donald's left, how are they sitting?

5. If O = 5 and TWO + TWO = FOUR, what do the other letters represent?

Week 28

1. How many triangles can you make on the grid below with a dot at each corner?

2. Each member of a rugby team (15 players) was asked to sign autographs. A minority refused but the others got on with the job so that each set of autographs was identical. There were 2607 signatures all told. How many players refused to sign?

3. What two numbers have a difference of 9 and a sum of 18?

4. Volumes 1 to 3 of a three-volume novel are tidily placed on a bookshelf. If the books are each 30 mm thick (including covers each 2 mm thick) what is the distance between the title page and the last page of the novel?

5. Find four consecutive whole numbers whose product is 3024.

Week 29

1. How many leaves of a book are there between page 8 and page 17?

2. Every member of a group shook hands with everyone else in the group. If there were 210 such welcomes, how many were in the group?

3. Can you place four identical coins so that each is touching the other three?

4. What is the largest possible number of children in a marbles group if no two children have the same number of marbles, there are more children than any child has marbles, and no children have 17 marbles?

5. I think of a two-digit number; if I subtract 5 it is a multiple of 4, if I subtract 6 it is a multiple of 5, if I subtract 7 it is a multiple of 6. What is the number?

Week 30

1.   I bought 17 plates (large and small) for $100. If the large plates cost $1 more than the small, what was the cost of each?

2.   Which two numbers have a sum of 10 and a difference of 20?

3.   A famous mathematician bought seven doughnuts and ate all but three. How many were left over?

4.   When Jansen retired he kept a quarter of his square farm and divided the rest between his four children. Each child was given a plot of the same size and shape. How?

5.   Find a two-digit number which is both a perfect square and a perfect cube.

Week 31

1.   Write down the next three symbols:

   ↑ 🙾 8 ⟰ 🗗

2.   How many triangles are there with each vertex that of a given heptagon?

3.   There is a hurdle every 10 metres of a 110 metre single running track. How many hurdles are there altogether?

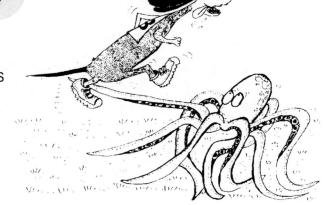

4.   Find 10 different ways to give change of $100. You may use $10, $20 and $50 notes.

*5.   In a field of cows, sheep and a lot of ducks, the number of sheep and ducks altogether totals three times the number of cows, while their heads and feet (without the cows) add up to 100. How many of each are there? Oh, and how many cows?

Week 32

*1. Which is more likely, a total of six with two dice, or six with one?

2. If $X^2 = OF$ and $(OX)^2 = OAF$, find the value of each letter.

*3. If you keep wagering half your money on the toss of a fair coin, do you expect in the long run to win, lose or come out even?

4. Mrs Ransome's farm was in the form of an equilateral triangle. She kept a quarter when she retired and divided the remainder between her four grandchildren, giving each a plot of the same size and shape. How?

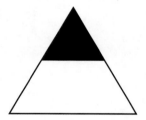

5. Alice has 15 oranges and Nancy 9. Karl has 16 apples which he will share between the other two if they will divide the oranges equally between the three of them. To be fair, how many apples should go to Alice and how many to Nancy?

Week 33

1. Draw four straight lines to isolate each of the crosses.

2. What is the largest number you can get using just four ones (no signs allowed)?

*3. Joe and Flo each throw a fair die. What are the chances that Joe's throw will be more than Flo's?

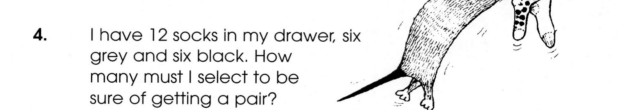

4. I have 12 socks in my drawer, six grey and six black. How many must I select to be sure of getting a pair?

5. An icon weighing 120 g is made of gold, bronze and tin. If the gold and bronze together weigh 90 g and the gold and tin together weigh 72 g, what is the weight of the gold?

Week 34

1. Complete the magic square with the whole numbers 3 to 9.
(Magic squares have the same sum for each row, column
and diagonal.)

		10
	11	

2. Wanda's age is three-quarters of Yolande's. In four years'
time it will be four-fifths. How old are the two girls?

3. There are two ducks in front of a duck, two ducks behind a
duck and a duck in the middle. What is the smallest
possible number of ducks?

4. On a racetrack one car travels at five laps a minute and
the other at eight laps a minute. If they start together, how
long is it before the second car laps the first?

*5. When extending my square courtyard, which was made up
of an even number of square tiles, I kept it square using
another 80 tiles. How many tiles were there in the courtyard
after I extended it?

Week 35

1.   Of those people in a New Zealand town who speak Maori or English, 10% speak Maori and 94% speak English. How many speak both Maori and English?

2.   Nikki, Heke and Mickey came first, second and third. The shortest, an only child, came second. Nikki, who is taller than the winner, married Heke's sister. Who won?

*3. It takes twice as long for a passenger train to pass a goods train going in the same direction as it would to pass it going in the opposite direction at the same speed. If the speed of the goods train is 30 km/h, what is the speed of the passenger train?

4.   Find $50 \div \frac{1}{2} + 3$.

*5. In the zonal hockey tournament, Australia won both games, scoring a total of three goals with one against. New Zealand won one and lost one with four goals for and against, while Fiji scored two goals with four against. Find the score in each game.

Week 36

1. Briar bought 1 at the hardware store for 20 cents, then 12 for 40 cents and finally 100 for 60 cents. What did she buy?

*2. $(XI)^2$ = CXXI in Roman numerals. If it is also true when the letters represent our own Arabic numerals, what are C, X and I?

3. How many triangles can you find?

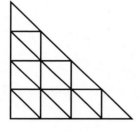

*4. Can you place two identical non-rectangular pieces of wood to form a rectangle either 6 cm by 2 cm or 4 cm by 3 cm?

5. If a 1-litre jug has its dimensions doubled, how many litres would the new jug hold?

Week 37

1. I had cards numbered 1 to 9 and dealt four piles each of two cards, keeping the last card. If the totals of each pair were 5, 7, 11 and 14, how were they made up?

2. Two kids collect soft drink cans to recycle for money. They know that if they collect 6 empty cans, they will receive 1 full can in exchange. If they gather 36 cans, how many drinks can they have between them?

3. There are 10 marbles of each of the colours red, green and yellow in a bag. How many must I select to be sure of getting two of each colour?

4. Miss Bones had a farm in the shape of a 45°, 45°, 90° triangle. When she retired she kept a quarter and left the rest to four relations so that each plot was of the same size and shape. How?

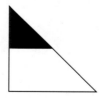

*5. If the output from (1,2) is 7, from (2,1) is 8, from (1,1) is 5 and from (2,2) is 10, what is the output from (2,3)? Hint: How many of each number in the pair do you need?

Week 38

1.   If Christmas Day is on a Thursday, how many Saturdays are there in the following January?

*2.   A drawer contains red socks and green socks. I need to pick out the same number of socks to be sure of getting a pair as I do to be sure of getting one sock of each colour. How many socks are there in the drawer?

3.   If $AA^2 = BCB$, find ABC.

4.   When four students picked up their assignments, each received an assignment belonging to one of the others. In how many ways can that happen?

5.   How many small squares are there on the faces of a Rubik's cube?

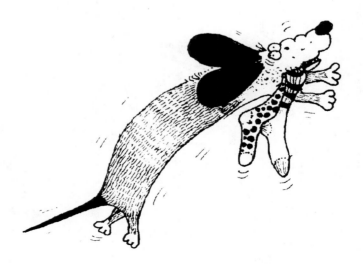

Week 39

1. If an aeroplane could fly right around the equator at a height of 1000 metres, how much further than the length of the equator would it have to fly?

2. Using a balance and a 2-gram weight, can you get 47 grams of sawdust from a 100-gram packet in just two weighings?

3. If $(DO)^3$ = DROP, what digit does each letter represent?

4. Two plumbers are watching a football match. One is the father of the other's daughter. Explain.

*5. In a game of billiards Avim normally gives Adit 20 points in every 100 (so Adit only needs 80 to win), while Adit gives Adunof 25 points in every hundred. What is the fair handicap when Avim plays Adunof?

Week 40

1. Mrs Bee cuts her cakes, some into thirds and some into quarters. How can she give equal amounts of her seven cakes to her twelve grandchildren?

*2. It rained on nine days of my holiday but only in the morning or the evening, never both. If there were seven fine mornings and eight fine evenings, how long was the holiday?

*3. How many squares can you find with each corner on a grid point of the five-by-five lattice?

● ● ● ● ●

● ● ● ● ●

● ● ● ● ●

● ● ● ● ●

● ● ● ● ●

*4. Barry's grandfather clock had wound down and he had no other means of telling the time. He went to his friend's house (where there was a clock) stayed a while and returned. Then he put his clock right. How?

5. I have a set of cubes, each one having some red and some blue sides, and every one different. How big can this set be?

Holiday stretch: Autumn

1A. Bill, Charlie and Don are married to Lucy, Merle and Nora, but not in that order. At a party none of them danced with their spouse; Bill danced with Merle, Don with Bill's wife and Don's wife with Merle's husband. Who was married to whom?

2A. Fill in the empty squares with positive integers to give the totals shown, without repeating a number in any row or column.

1	2	3	6
		1	7
			8
			9
10	10	10	

3A. Liston is due west of Marfield and due north of Newdle. Otway is midway berween Marfield and Newdle which are 10 km apart. How far is it from Liston to Otway?

4A. The grid below shows the centre and vertices of a regular hexagon. How many different triangles can be formed if each vertex is a point on the grid?

● ●

● ● ●

● ●

5A. Two large jars contain equal volumes of liquid, one of tea and the other of coffee. If half the coffee is poured into the tea and mixed thoroughly, and one third of the mixture is poured back into the coffee, is there more tea in the coffee or more coffee in the tea?

Holiday stretch: Autumn

*6A. The following product is always true in Roman numerals. Can you find different values of C, I, L and V which make it true in Arabic numerals (a) if C is odd and (b) if C is even?

$$\begin{array}{r} LI \\ \times \quad IV \\ \hline CCIV \end{array}$$

7A. You have 1 kg of sugar, a 200-gram weight, a balance and a set of identical containers. Use just two separate weighings to obtain exactly 100 grams of sugar.

8A. There are 12 pentomino shapes (five equal squares placed edge to edge). Here are four of them. How can you combine the S, V, C and P pentominoes to make a five-by-four rectangle?

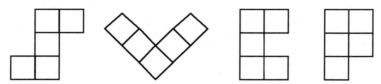

*9A. Find the smallest positive integer which has a remainder of 2 when divided by 4, a remainder of 4 when divided by 7 and a remainder of 6 when divided by 9.

*10A. 45 marbles are in four unequal piles. The product of the number of marbles in each pile is 7000. Find the number of marbles in each pile.

Holiday stretch: Winter

1W. Fill in the empty squares with positive integers to give the totals shown, without repeating a number in any row or column.

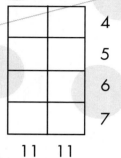

2W. A rectangular card 7 cm by 3 cm is divided by one straight cut so that the two pieces can be combined with a square of side 2 cm to form a larger square. How?

3W. Two cars climb and descend a hill – a distance of 1 km each side. The first car climbs at 30 km/h and descends at 90 km/h, while the second climbs and descends at a steady 50 km/h. Which car finishes first and by what distance?

4W. Find the greatest number of regions formed if 4 points are placed on a circle and each point is joined to all of the others. Now repeat with 5 points, then 6 points.

5W. Combine the W, P, T and V pentominoes to make a five-by-four rectangle.

   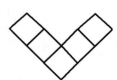

Holiday stretch: Winter

*6W. If each letter stands for a different non-zero digit, find GO and STOP.

$$
\begin{array}{r}
GO \\
\times\ GO \\
\hline
STOP
\end{array}
$$

7W. Alex, Jan and Pat were a painter, a secretary and a teacher. Jan met the teacher who was a bridesmaid at Pat's wedding. What was Alex's occupation?

8W. The hour and minute hand are together at noon. When were they last together?

*9W. Find the smallest positive integer which has remainders of 2, 3 and 4 when divided by 5, 7 and 11 respectively.

*10W. Find three distinct positive integers a, b and c such that:
$15a + 21b + 35c = 310$

Holiday stretch: Spring

1P. In a hall meeting, 55% of those present were men and the same number were graduates. If one-fifth of the men and all except for two of the women were graduates, how many people were there in the hall?

2P. Fill in the empty squares with positive integers to give the totals shown, without repeating a number in any row or column, or the two centre diagonals.

1	2	3	5	11
		1		11
				11
				11
11	11	11	11	11

3P. Neddie bought odd numbers of 35c and 45c stamps and spent exactly $10. How many of each did he buy?

4P. An equilateral triangle surrounds a circle of radius 10 cm, and is itself surrounded by a larger circle (as shown). Find the radius of this circle.

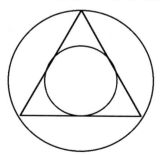

5P. What is the largest possible value of coins it is possible to have without having any coins which will add to exactly $4? (Coins are 5c, 10c, 20c, 50c, $1, $2.)

Holiday stretch: Spring

6P.   Combine the F, L, Y and C pentominoes to make a 5 by 4 rectangle:

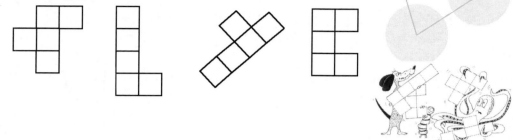

7P.   Find three whole numbers with a sum of 26 and a product of 84.

8P.   Abi, Ebi and Ubi come from three different tribes: the Pert, who are truthful; the Quert, who always tell lies; and the Zert, who alternate truth and lie. When I asked which tribe they were from, they gave the following replies:
Abi: 'Ebi is not a Pert; Ubi is a Quert.'
Ebi: 'Ubi is a Pert; Abi is a Pert.'
Ubi: 'Abi is a Quert; Ebi is not a Zert.'
What was the tribe of each?

9P.   In Roman numerals, IV + IV + IV = XII. Find I, V and X if this is true using Arabic numerals.

*10P.   How many oblongs are there with all corners on the grid shown?

Holiday stretch: Summer

*1U. Fill in the empty squares with integers 1 to 5 to give the totals shown, without repeating a number in any row or column, or the two centre diagonals.

6	7	8	9	30
				14
				12
				11
17	15	17	18	17 13

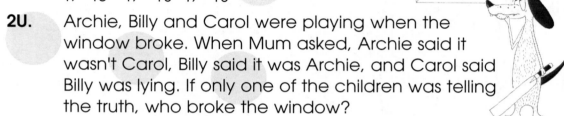

2U. Archie, Billy and Carol were playing when the window broke. When Mum asked, Archie said it wasn't Carol, Billy said it was Archie, and Carol said Billy was lying. If only one of the children was telling the truth, who broke the window?

3U. My watch, which loses 3 minutes a day, and my bedroom clock, which gains 2 minutes a day, gave the same time at noon on 1 January 2005. On what 2 other dates of the same year did they give the same (12 hour) time?

4U. How many triangles?

5U. A rectangular billiard table 200 cm by 150 cm, with perfectly reflecting cushions, has four pockets (one at each corner) and markers along each side at intervals of 50 cm. If the ball is placed 50 cm from two adjacent sides (as shown), which of the labelled markers should you aim at if the ball is not to end up in a pocket? (A, D, H and K are forbidden.)

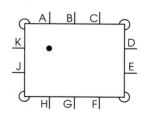

Holiday stretch: Summer

6U. Stamps are sold in multiples of 5c values. Chico bought 7 of one value and 11 of another, spending exactly $5. Find the values of the stamps.

7U. Complete the magic square with positive odd numbers so that each row, column and diagonal adds up to 39.

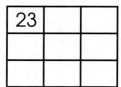

8U. A cuboid has a volume of 120 cm^3 and the total length of the edges is 1 m. What are its dimensions?

9U. Combine the L, I, P and Z pentominoes to make a 10-by-2 rectangle.

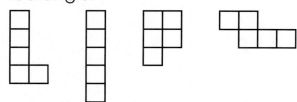

*10U. Dorham, Exington and Farrar are three towns whose soccer teams play each other home and away. The season's results are shown in the incomplete table below. Given that a home win earns 2 points, an away win 3 points and a draw 1 point for the home team and 2 points for the away team, and that Farrar drew a home game, see if you can find the results of all six games.

	W	D	L	Points	
Farrar		2			6
Exington			2		5
Dorham				2	4

Stretchers answers

Week 1

1. **74,** since each match eliminates one player.
    (Round 1: 37, round 2: 19, round 3: 9, round 4: 5, round 5: 2, round 6: 1,
    final: 1 – work systematically.)

2. **Alison.** By elimination, the arrangement is (clockwise) Alison, Pat, Tania, Betty; hence
    Alison drives neither the van nor the truck.
    Note: Problems of the sort 'Who has which occupation?' can often be simplified using
    a chart or diagram:

    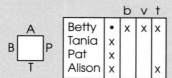

    Pat is on Tania's right so Tania drives the van. The rest falls into place.

3. **The sum of the lengths of two sides of a triangle is always greater than
    that of the third.** Otherwise the shortest distance between two points would not be a
    straight line!

4. **B.**

    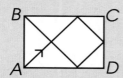

5. **E = 6, I = 5, N = 8, W = 2.** W must be 1 or 2 (NEW has only three digits), but if
    W = 1, then E = 3 × 1 = 3 and N = 3 × 3 = 9, which makes W = 2! Hence W = 2,
    E = 6, N = 8 and I = 4 + 1 = 5. 3 × 862 = 2586.
    Note: This is an example of an *alphametic*, the representation of the digits of a
    numerical question and its solution by different letters. It is a convention that no number
    may start with a zero and every letter stands for a different digit. Some alphametics
    have their letters form a keyword when the digits are placed in order 0 to 9.
    Obviously if there are, say, seven different letters (with over half a million combinations
    possible), trial is not a sound strategy; to reduce the workload, there are a number of
    digit properties worth noting.
    ### Addition
    The sum of two digits can have a 'carry' of 1 at the most.
    The sum of two identical digits is even.
    If 0 is added to a digit to give a new digit, there must be a carry figure.
    If 0 is in the total there is a carry to the next column.
    Subtractions can be rewriten as additions.
    ### Multiplication
    If A × A = __ A, then A = 0 or 1 (no carry) or 5 (carry 2) or 6 (carry 3).
    If ABC × D = ABC, then D = 1.
    If A × B = C, the only possibilities are
    A = 4 and B = 2; A = 3 and B = 2; A = 2 and B = 3 or 4.
    (The same holds true if A, B ≠ 1 and A × B ≤ C.)

If A × B = __ 1, then
A = 3 and B = 7
or A = 7 and B = 3.
If A × B = A, then A = 0 or B = 1
If A × B = __ A, then
A = 5 and B is odd
or B = 6 and A is even.
The sum of digits of a multiple of 3 (or 9) is itself a multiple of 3 (or 9).
Long multiplication shows a multiplication for each digit.
Long division shows a multiplication for each digit of the quotient.
Division can be rewritten as a multiplication (with an addition if there is a remainder).

Week 2

1.   **Thursday.** It helps to use remainders after dividing by 7 (called modulo 7 or 7-clock arithmetic) on this sort of problem. A normal year has 52 weeks and one day (remainder 1), and the monthly remainders are 3, 0, 3, 2, 3, 2, 3, 3, 2, 3, 2, 3 respectively. If, for example, you are reading this on Wednesday, 4 October 2006, the remainder is:
     2 (leap year) + 1 + 21 (Jan. – Oct.) + 3 = 27 = 6 (modulo 7), giving 6 days before Wednesday. (Look for pattern; solve a simpler problem.)

2.   **A = 3, B = 9, C = 6.** Since BB has only two digits, A must be 1, 2 or 3. It is not 1, since A × A ≠ A + A while 1 × 1 = 1; nor 2, since A × A ≠ A + A while 2 × 2 = 2 + 2. Hence A = 3. 33 × 3 = 99, 33 + 3 = 36. (Work systematically – see W1/5.)

3.   **A and C are Fixers, B is a Goodie.** From the first statement, A is not a Goodie. If B is a Fixer and thus lying, C would have to be a Fixer too – impossible since A is lying. So B is a Goodie, and C is a fixer. (Use reasoning, make a chart.)
     Note: Statements which involve telling the truth and lying have double information. Test (a) whether the speaker is lying and (b) what the speaker says. In this and succeeding questions about the island of Koo, every complete statement by a Goodie is true, and every complete statement by a Fixer is false. Thus if a Goodie says 'A and B are both Fixers', they are; but if a Fixer says 'A and B are both Fixers', then at least one of A and B is not a Fixer.

4.   **ABC.** Each of the marked diagonals has equal length. (Draw a diagram.)

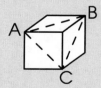

5.   **1, 5 and 15.** The prime factors of 75 are 3, 5, 5, but these add to 13, so one child must be 1 year old and the others 3 and 25 (which gives an incorrect total) or 5 and 15. (Guess and check.)

Week 3

1. **8.** If 2 of the triangles each contain 2 sides of the decagon, the remaining part is an octagon; repeating the process with 2 more triangles as sides of the octagon we have a hexagon, then a quadrilateral which is 2 triangles. By taking one side as the base and joining to each vertex in turn, any convex polygon of *n* sides can be formed using (*n* – 2) triangles. (Draw a diagram.)

2. **59 minutes.** (Use reasoning.)

3. **14 stamps.** Jim and June are not a couple, since there are no whole numbers which add to 30 and differ by 5. Since Janet bought 9, Jim bought 21, June 16 and hence John 14. (Work systematically.)

4. **30.** Polly knew $\frac{5}{6}$ by their face, so $\frac{1}{6}$ by name only. (Venn diagrams can be useful for this sort of problem.)

5. **8 cm by 5 cm.** A little thought shows that the cuts must be made as shown. (Work backwards.)

Week 4

1. This is one alternative. It seems that 7 trees can usually be isolated in this way. It makes an interesting investigation to find arrangements of trees which cannot be thus isolated. (Solve a simpler problem.)

2. **9 kg.** Two thirds of its weight is 6 kg.

3. **1 and 5, 2 and 3.** If the sums were 10 and 3 the pair whose sum is 3 would be 1 and 2, so the pair whose sum is 10 and product is 9 must be 1 and 9; these numbers are not all distinct. Hence the sums are 6 and 5.
    2 and 4 give no possible distinct numbers whose sum is 5, so 6 = 1 + 5 and 5 = 2 + 3. (Guess and check.)

4. **D and E are both Fixers.** D cannot be a Goodie, so is lying; hence E is not a Goodie. (Use reasoning – see W 2/3.)

5. **44%.** The first device uses 70% of the fuel, while the second uses 80% of that, or 56% altogether. No, you can't add – what if each saved 60%? (Solve a simpler problem.)

Week 5

1.   **16.** The remainder on division by 9 is the sum of the digits, taken more than once if needed. $4 + 4 + 4 + 4 = 16$, $1 + 6 = 7$. Since $18 = 2 \times 9$, the remainder after division by 18 must be either 7 or 16. We reject 7 as it is an odd number, while 4444 and 18 are even.

2.   **Take the second full glass, pour the contents into the second empty glass and return it (now empty) to its former position.** (Act it out.)

3.   **12.** Only the middle-edge cubes are painted on two sides, and there are 12 edges. (Draw a diagram; make a model.)

4.   **6.** There are 4 small squares, the large square and the square shown. (Work systematically.)

5.   **1.** Apart from (2, 2, 2), no partition of 6 into three whole numbers (e.g. 1, 2, 3) has the largest number less than the sum of the other two. Investigate further with 7, 8, 9 … matches. (Make a model – see W 1/3.)

Week 6

1.   **Peter used five 7-cm rods and Marilyn used four 9-cm rods.**

    By tabulation,

Peter	7	14	21	28	35	42
Marilyn	9	18	27	36		

    The next highest solution, 98 and 99, requires more than ten rods each. This sort of problem leads to a simple Diophantine (integer) equation:

$$9m - 7p = 1$$

    where Marilyn has m rods and Peter p rods. (Guess and check; look for a pattern.)

2.   **After A backs up, B uncouples its second carriage, goes forward then back on to the siding (see diagram 1), and A goes through, coupling up to B's second carriage. The shortened train B goes some distance on to the main line (diagram 2); A backs up, uncouples B's second carriage on to the siding (diagram 3) and moves off. Finally B backs up to its second carriage and moves off complete with both carriages (diagram 4).** (Make a model)

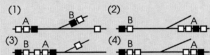

3.   **PLEA = 2198.** From the thousands L = 1 and there must be a 'carry' from the hundreds, so $2 \times E = 10 + E$ (impossible) or $2 \times E + 1 = 10 + E$, giving E = 9; from the units P = $2 \times$ L, so P = 2.
    $991 + 991 = 1982$. (Work systematically – see W 1/5.)

---

4. **Never!** The Rifles go three paces while the Fusiliers go two, so they will only be together when the Fusiliers have gone an even number of paces and have their right feet down. (Act it out.)

5. **6 cm by 3 cm.** If the dimensions in centimetres are a and b, then

$$ab = 2(a + b)$$

so $$a(b - 2) = 2b$$

and $$a = \frac{2b}{b-2}$$

a is a whole number if b = 3, 4 or 6 (by trial), but we reject b = 4 which would give a square. (Form an equation.)

Week 7

1. $(a + b)^2 = a^2 + b^2 + 2ab > a^2 + b^2$, since $a, b > 0$. Geometrically, $(a + b)$ is the whole square, while $a^2 + b^2$ is the shaded portion.
(Form an equation; draw a diagram.)

2. **43.** If all members had given a donation, receipts in dollars would be $301 = 7 \times 43$. Hence the subscription was $6 with a $1 donation. (Make a chart; look for a pattern.)

3. $5\frac{5}{11}$ **minutes past 1.** The minute hand passes the hour hand 11 times in 12 hours, since the minute hand travels twelve revolutions while the hour hand travels one. Hence the hour hand has travelled $\frac{1}{11}$ of a revolution which is $5\frac{5}{11}$ minute divisions. Alternatively, the minute hand gains 55 minute divisions every hour, so it will gain 60 minute divisions (and thus be together with the hour hand again) in $\frac{60}{55}$ hours = 1 hour $5\frac{5}{11}$ minutes. (Use reasoning; make a model.)

4. **6.** The centres of the surrounding coins form a regular hexagon, with each side formed by 2 radii. (Make a model.)

5. **None.** We already have 77% + 71% − 48% = 100% counted. (Draw a Venn diagram.)

Week 8

1. The four extra triangles double the area of the square. (Draw a diagram.)

2. **3 and 37.** This is easy to see since the digits add to a multiple of 3, so 3 is a divisor (see W 1/5). (A pleasant trick with 37 is to press any three digits in a straight line on a calculator then press in reverse order. The result is always a multiple of 37, e.g. 852258 = 37 × 23034. Why?)

---

3.   **5.** The interesting point about this problem is that each combination (4 red; 3 red and 1 green; 2 red and 2 green; 1 red and 3 green; 4 green) can only be painted in one way. (Make a model.)

4.   **10.** 90 games are played, so even if every member played two games there are 10 games unaccounted for. (Use reasoning; make a chart; solve a simpler problem.)

5.   **6.** It cannot be done with three sectors of one colour, so there must be 2 sectors of one colour, 2 of a second and 1 of a third. If the single colour is orange and we start with that, there are only OGBGB and OBGBG. With three colours to choose from for the single sector there are thus 3×2 arrangements possible. Three of these are reflections of the other three. (Draw a diagram; work systematically.)

Week 9

1.   **120 ways.** The first letter can be any one of five; once this is selected, there are four choices for the second, then three for the third, two for the second and only one (no choice) for the last. Hence there are $5 \times 4 \times 3 \times 2 \times 1$ choices all told. (Make a model.)

2.   **22.** The next round must have 64 entries, so 11 must be eliminated. In any knock-out competition the number of matches in a preliminary round will be the number of entrants less the power of two immediately less than this. This ensures there will be no 'byes' later. (Make a chart; work backwards.)

3.   **3 spiders and 5 beetles.** You can use simultaneous equations – or just keep on subtracting 8 till you are left with a multiple of 6 (54, 46, 38, 30). (Guess and check; make a chart.)

4.   **Alec.** Alec and Beth contradicted one another so one was lying. Therefore Charlie told the truth.(Use reasoning.)

5.   **27 hexagons** (3 + 4 + 5 + 4 + 3 = 19 unit hexagons, 2 + 3 + 2 = 7 doubles, 1 triple). (Look for a pattern; work systematically.)

Week 10

1.   **2 girls.** If numbers 2, 4 and 6 had blue eyes, then the fair-haired girls were 1 and 4, 2 and 5, or 3 and 6. In each case there are just four girls with one or the other attribute. (Draw a diagram.)

2.   **$5.** The camera, of course, cost $105. (Guess and check.)

3.   **3 ways.** Just one colour is used on two (adjacent) faces and there are three colours. Try it. (Make a model.)

4.   **H said 'Fixer'.** If the word had been 'Goodie', either both were Goodies or both Fixers. (Use reasoning – see W 2/3.)

5.   **1.25 litres.** The 3 cm of air and the 5 cm of liquid are both cylinders, so the bottle is equivalent to a cylinder 8 cm high. (Use reasoning; draw a diagram.)

Week 11

1. **9.** A perfect square cannot be negative; 9 is obtained when I think of $-\frac{1}{2}$

2. **23.** Receipts from subscriptions alone are $299 = 23 \times $13. (Make a chart; look for a pattern – see W 7/2.)

3. **$3.50.** Working backwards, Troll had $(0 + 4) ÷ 2 = $2 after paying the second toll, $(2 + 4) ÷ 2 = $3 after the first and $(3 + 4) ÷ 2 = $3.50 to start with. Alternatively, if Troll starts with x, the effect is:
$$x \rightarrow 2x - 4 \rightarrow 2(2x - 4) - 4 = 4x - 12 \rightarrow 2(4x - 12) - 4$$
Hence $8x - 28 = 0$. (Work backwards.)

4. **130 cm.** Imagine the cylinder's curved surface unrolled twice. The string will then be a straight line and Pythagoras's theorem used. (Make a model.)

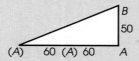

5. **161.** Successive differences are 4, 12, 36, __, __, each 3 times the one before. If the pattern is continued, 108, 324 … the next figures would be 53 + 108 = 161 + 324 = 485, confirming the hunch.
(Work systematically; guess and check.)

Week 12

1. **4 km/h.** Beware of adding averages! If the hill is 6 km long, the time taken will be $\frac{6}{3} + \frac{6}{6} = 3$ hours. Hence her average speed is $\frac{12}{3}$ km/h. The result is the same whatever the length of the hill. (Guess and check.)

2. **60 and 13.** Note that $\sqrt{(x^2 y^2)} = xy$, but $\sqrt{(x^2 + y^2)} \neq x + y$.

3. **4 times.** They will meet when Bradley has run $\frac{3}{5}$ and Mark $\frac{2}{5}$ of a circuit, and again at $(\frac{6}{5}, \frac{4}{5})$, $(\frac{9}{5}, \frac{6}{5})$ and $(\frac{12}{5}, \frac{8}{5})$ before finishing together. Alternatively, Bradley can be considered as going round five times relative to Mark (i.e. with Mark stationary) giving the same result. (Act it out.)

4. **K is a fixer, L a Weasel and M a Goodie.** If K (not a Goodie) is telling the truth, L would be a Goodie and hence M a Fixer telling the truth! K must be lying and a Fixer, with L also lying. (Use reasoning – see W 2/3.)

5. **Yes: form the matches into a double tetrahedron.** (Make a model.)

Week 13

1. **61.** In general the *n*th odd number is $(2n - 1)$ – double the number and subtract 1.

2. **125 cm.** Because the fish turned a right angle, it finished at the opposite end of the diameter. Pythagoras again! (Draw a diagram.)

3. **4 different bracelets.** (This assumes that the bracelet looks the same from both sides; if not, the answer is 6.)
    Reds together and green together: RRGGB   1 way
    Reds together or green together RRGBG, GGRBR   2 ways
    All separate GRGRB   1 way
    If the reverse order is counted as different, add GGRRB, RGRGB. (Draw a diagram; work systematically.)

4.   or

    (Other patterns are variations, reversing the side numbers, or rotating or reflecting the figure). Note that the numbers 1 to 9 plus the corner numbers add to 69, and the numbers alone add to 45, so the corners must be 7, 8, 9 since their sum is 24. (Guess and check; look for a pattern.)

5. **No, just clever!** Some days are counted twice and some do not have 24 hours. Try to remove the paradox. (Work systematically.)

Week 14

1. **8.** Many people say 6 without thinking. Counting the faces, corners and edges of a solid figure with plane faces demonstrates the Euler (pronounced 'Oiler') relation: faces + corners = edges + 2. For the cube, there are 6 faces, 8 corners and 12 edges. (Make a model.)

2. **Peter had 14 oysters, Sarah 84.** 'Guess and check' will get the answer, but algebra is probably quicker. If Peter has *x* oysters, then for Sarah:
    $98 - 4x = \frac{1}{2}(98 - x)$
    from which $x = 14$.

3. **2 hours,** assuming you take one immediately. (Make a chart.)

4. **N is a Goodie, P a Fixer.** If N were a Fixer, N would be lying and no-one would be a Fixer. This is a contradiction. (Use reasoning – see W 2/3.)

5. **80 minutes = 1 hour 20 minutes.** (Draw a diagram.)

Week 15

1. **12 seconds.** There are 12 intervals between the flags, so the seventh flag (six intervals) is at halfway. (Draw a diagram.)

2. **2 revolutions.** Suprisingly, philosophers and sages have argued different answers over the centuries; an experiment should quickly convince. (Make a model.)

3. **47.** They can now count in base nine, with digits 1, 2, 4, 5, 6, 7, 8, 9, 0. (Work systematically.)

4. **C = 3, V = 9, I = 7.** CCC must be a multiple of 111 and so of 37 (see W 8/2); CI is not 74 since 777 is odd. 37 × 9 = 333. (Work systematically.)

5. **18 triangles.** There are three possible apices (plural of 'apex') in the top line, each of which can be joined to the three possible bases on the bottom line, making nine triangles; the other nine have their base on the top line and apex on the bottom line. (Work systematically.)

Week 16

1. **15, 5, 25.** Twice the sum of the side numbers must be 90. Their sum is 45 and the numbers are 45 − 30, 45 − 40 and 45 − 20. (Guess and check; look for a pattern.)

2. **1.** After 2, all even numbers are multiples of 2, so are not a prime.

3. **11.** Only February has fewer.

4. **Give the last child a dollar in the purse.**

5. **$3.50.** After 2 crossings Troll has $(0 ÷ 2) + 2 = $2, after 1 crossing $(2 ÷ 2) + 2 = $3, and he starts with $(3 ÷ 2) + 2 = $3.50.
Alternatively, if the Troll starts with $x, then:
$x \rightarrow 2(x - 2) = 2x - 4 \rightarrow 2(2x - 6) = 4x - 12 \rightarrow 2(4x - 14)$
So $4x - 14 = 0$. (Work backwards – see W 11/3.)

Week 17

1. **62.** Two less than the wanted number has factors 3, 4, 5 and 6. The only such number with two digits is 60.

2. **10 triangles.** 5 straight lines can have 10 points of intersection. From the figure, triangles are formed from *ABE; ACF; ADG; BCH; BDI; CDJ; EFH; EGI; FGJ; HIJ.* (Draw a diagram.)

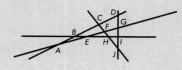

3. **My son.** My father's son must be me. (Use reasoning.)

4. **The bottom part of the flange,** which is below the rail on which the wheel is rolling; hence it is going backwards when the train is going forwards. (Draw a diagram.)

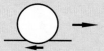

5. **7 cars and 4 trucks.** There must be an even number of trucks to keep the dollar sum even. Try 0, 2, 4, 6, 8 trucks; then the amounts left for cars are $100, $78, $56, $34, $12. Only $56 is a multiple of $8. This is another Diophantine equation:
    $8c + 11t = 100$.
    The only solution in whole numbers is $c = 7$, $t = 4$. (Guess and check.)

Week 18

1. **A = 5, B = 1, C = 2.** From $A^2 = CA$, A must be 5 or 6, and since $35^2 > 1000$, B is 1 or 2. Only $15^2 = 225$ meets the CCA pattern. (Work systematically – see W 1/5.)

2. **Hold the cube at two opposite corners and bisect.** The cut will pass through all six faces symmetrically. (Make a model.)

3. **35 triangles.** There are 5 triangles each using two edges of the pentagon, $5 \times 4 = 20$ triangles each using just one edge, 5 using a diagonal but no edges and 5 'star-points'. (Work systematically; look for a pattern.)

4. $\frac{1}{3}$. If the fraction is $\frac{x}{y}$, then:
    $$\frac{x+3}{y+3} = \frac{2x}{y}$$
    $$xy + 3y = 2xy + 6x$$
    $$3y - xy = 6x$$
    $$y = \frac{6x}{3-x}$$
    The only solutions in whole numbers are:
    $x = 1$, $y = 3$ and $x = 2$, $y = 12$
    and only the first gives a fraction in lowest terms. (Form an equation.)

5. **50%.** Since the mark-up is 20%, sale price is $\frac{120}{100} \times$ cost price and $\frac{80}{100} \times$ normal selling price. Hence normal selling price is $\frac{120}{100} \times \frac{100}{80} = \frac{3}{2} \times$ cost price. (Work backwards.)

Week 19

1.

---

2.   **8.48.** The hour hand is on an exact minute division at 0, 12, 24, 36 and 48 minutes past the hour, giving 0-, 1-, 2-, 3- and 4-division leads to the minute hand respectively over the appropriate hour at 12.00, 2.12, 4.24, 6.36 and 8.48. (Guess and check; look for a pattern – see W 7/3.)

3.   **The same distance.** One purpose of these questions is to start discussions, and the meaning of 'meet' will arise without a doubt. 'Meet' is assumed here to mean 'are exactly opposite'.

4.   **26.** Actually there can be no definitively correct answer as we are not told the pattern. The answer given here is obtained by noting that first differences between successive terms are 1, 2, 4, 7..., and second differences are thus 1, 2, 3...; continuing the pattern gets the answer given. This sequence is formed by:

$\frac{1}{6}n(n-1)(n-2) + n$, with $n = 1, 2, 3...$

However a less simple alternative could be the sequence formed by:

$$2^{n-1} - \frac{1}{24}(n-1)(n-2)(n-3)(n-4)$$

which for $n = 1, 2, 3...$ is:

$1 - 0, 2 - 0, 4 - 0, 8 - 0, 16 - 1, 32 - 5...$

i.e $1, 2, 4, 8, 15, 27 ...$! (Work systematically.)

5.   **S is a Fixer, T a Goodie.** If S were a Goodie, T would be telling the truth, so also a Goodie. T actually said S was not a Goodie. (Use reasoning – see W 2/3.)

Week 20

1.   **6 ways.**

Each colour on opposite faces:	1 way
One colour on opposite faces (R, G or B)	3 ways
All colours on adjacent faces	2 ways

The last two are mirror images of each other. (Make a model.)

2.   **4 screws.** (Guess and check; make a chart.)

No. of screws	Unit cost	10c less	2 more	New cost
1	$1.20	$1.10	3	$3.30
2	$0.60	$0.50	4	$2.00
3	$0.40	$0.30	5	$1.50
4	$0.30	$0.20	6	$1.20

3.   **6 cm.** The original 1 cm of oil transfers to the sleeve and, as the cylinder rises 1 cm, the sleeve will have 2 cm of oil. This transfers back to the cylinder when the stroke is completed so the cylinder also has 2 cm of oil. The process repeats for the five strokes. You can notice this apparently odd phenomenon when walking in mud; as your gumboots rub, the mudline gets higher! (Draw several diagrams.)

4.   **A is Gibble, B is Gobble.** Either both are lying (impossible since they lie on different days) or they are both telling the truth and it is Saturday. (Use reasoning – see W2/3.)

5.   **The chances are $\frac{1}{3}$.** The remaining possibilities, all equally likely, are (girl, girl), (girl, boy) and (boy, girl).

Week 21

1. **4 minutes.** In 12 minutes the hot tap could fill 1 bath and the cold tap 2 baths, so together they could fill 3 baths. (Draw a diagram.)

2. **Kite, parallelogram.** No side can be 3 or more matches long since the other 3 sides would have a maximum of three between them. Hence the partition of 6 must be (2, 2, 1, 1) or (2, 1, 2, 1) or an equivalent. (Make a model – see W 1/3.)

3. **Tui and Dan eat all three; Alison won't eat any.** Since Tui and Dan must both eat toast, Alison won't eat cereal either. (Work systematically.)

4. **BA^2 = CCA.** A must be 1, otherwise the square would make a higher hundreds figure; the only squares between 100 and 200 are 100 (rejected since B ≠ C), 121, 144, 169 and 196. Only 144 has the right pattern. Reversed, 21^2 = 441. (Use reasoning; work systematically – see W 1/5.)

5. **13, 8, 20.** Twice the sum of the corner numbers is 82, their sum is 41 and each is 41 – 28, 41 – 33 and 41 – 21. (Guess and check; look for a pattern.)

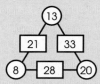

Week 22

1. **$1, $3, $4, $5 and $7.** The minimum amounts of $1, $3, $4, $5 and $6 add to $19, so the last amount is $(6 + 1) = $7. (Use reasoning.)

2. **20.** Ten are needed for the ones: 9, 19…; ten for the tens: 90, 91… (Work systematically.)

3.

4. **9 diamonds.** There are 4 plus the big one of type A, and 2 of each types of B and C. (Work systematically.)

5. **5 ships.** The ship from Auckland will meet those that left Sydney two days earlier and one day earlier as well as those which will leave Sydney while on its journey. (Make a chart.)

Week 23

1. **After 10 days.** 50 cm × 2 × 2 = 2 m. (Use reasoning.)

2. **F is a Fixer, G a Goodie.** F is obviously not a Goodie, so is lying; hence G is a Goodie. (Use reasoning – see W2/3.)

3. **9 children.** There can be 10 or 11, but there must be 9 or more. The heads and feet mentioned belong to the same children of course! (Draw a diagram.)

4. **1 minute 30 seconds.** Fry side 1 of steaks A and B, then side 2 of A with side 1 of C, then side 2 of B and C.

5. **She cost me $2.** 60 tomatoes at $1.50 for 5 yields $18, while 20 at 5 for $1 yields $4, and 40 at 5 for $2 yields $16 (making a total of $20). (Work systematically.)

Week 24

1. **81.** She must be 49, 64, 81 or 100, and 49 and 64 can hardly be considered old for a grandmother. If my parents' ages are x and y years old, then $(x + y)(x - y) =$ one of those numbers. For 100, x and y would be 26 and 24, too young to have such a venerable mother. For 64 they would be 17 and 15 and I wouldn't be posing the problem. (49 does actually have a sensible answer: 25 and 24.) Hence the answer, with my parents being 41 and 40. (15 and 12 also give the required difference – but really!) (Form an equation.)

2. **11.** Working backwards from *B* we can add the number of possible approaches from points nearer *B*. Alternatively, work forwards from *A*.

3. **Put 1 each in two of the corners, and arrange the others along the sides.** If the corners are opposite, have 4 of the remaining 16 along each side; if adjacent distribute 3, 4, 5, 4. You can even put both in the same corner with a 3, 5, 5, 3 distribution. (Draw a diagram.)
   If you wish, you could put an equal number of extra pots in each corner.

4. **41.** There is no definitive answer, but the numbers are alternate primes; hence 5, (7), 11, (13), 17, (19), 23, (29), 31, (37), 41. (Work systematically – see W 19/4.)

5. **5.** If the number is x we have $\frac{2x + 10}{2} - x = 5$ for any x. (Guess and check; form an equation.)

Week 25

1. **3 and 11.** The problem leads to Goldbach's conjecture that every even number greater than 6 can be written as the sum of two primes. Although not proven, most even numbers have many such sums, e.g. $34 = 3 + 31 = 5 + 29 = 11 + 23$. ($17 + 17$ is the same prime counted twice.) (Guess and check.)

2. **11.** Your first 10 could be 2 of each of the 5 colours. (Make a model.)

3. **Hold it by 2 opposite edges and bisect.** The resulting figure cuts each face symmetrically, joining midpoints of the other 4 edges. (Make a model.)

4. **Q and R are both Weasels.** They contradict each other, so cannot be both Goodies or both Fixers. Hence Q is a Weasel, and lying – otherwise R would be a Goodie and lying. R is thus telling the truth, but is not a Goodie. (Use reasoning; make a chart – see W2/3.)

5. **Both the sums and differences repeat the original sequence, though with different starts.** The sequence obeys the Fibonacci rule that each term is the sum of the previous two terms. Any initial numbers can be used and the result will hold. The Fibonacci sequence itself starts with 0 and 1. (Be observant!)

Week 26

1. **Alice is the oldest, then Alexander, then Arran.** If Alice were the youngest, Arran would not be and Alice would be the oldest. If Alexander were the youngest, Arran would not be and Alice would. Hence Arran is the youngest. (Use reasoning – see W1/2).

2. **459.** Call the original digits a, b and c. We then have:

$$
\begin{array}{r}
c \quad\quad b \quad\quad a \\
-\ a \quad\quad b \quad\quad c \\
\hline
c-a-1 \quad\quad 9 \quad\quad 10+a-c
\end{array}
$$
(since $c > a$)

If $b = 9$, $a = c - a - 1$ and $c = 10 + a - c$

$c = 2a + 1$ and $a = 2c - 10$

$c = 2(2c - 10) + 1$

$3c = 19$ so there is no whole number solution.

Hence $c = 9$ ($c > a$, remember) and

$a = c - a - 1$

$a = 8 - a$

$2a = 8$

$a = 4$

and $b = 10 + a - c = 5$.

$954 - 459 = 495$.

(Work systematically; form an equation.)

3. **3 links.** The blacksmith breaks all the links of one chain and uses them to join the other four. (Draw a diagram.)

4. If AB is $\frac{2}{3}$ metre, then the lengths of BC and PQ are both $\frac{2\sqrt{2}}{3}$ m, so 1-m planks will work – just! It is an interesting exercise requiring surds and Pythagoras to show that $AB = \frac{2}{3}$ metre. (Make a model.)

5. **No.** it will be midnight 3 days later.

Week 27

1. **28.** If the number is increased by 2 it will be divisible by 5 and 6.

2. **7900.** Since 25 = 100 ÷ 4, we can divide 316 by 4 (i.e. halve it twice) and multiply by 100.

3. **11.** My first ten could all be left gloves, 5 black and 5 white. (Work systematically.)

4. **The clockwise order is: Alice, Cara, Donald, Bill.** Neither Bill nor Donald is to Cara's right, so Alice is; Bill is thus opposite Cara. (Draw a diagram.)

5. **F = 1, R = 0, T = 7, U = 3, W = 6.** From the units column R = 0, and from the thousands F = 1 and there is a 'carry' from the hundreds, so T = 7. Since there is also a carry from the units, U is odd; U is not 9 (since W would also be 9), so U = 3, giving W = 6. 765 + 765 = 1530. (Work systematically – see W 1/5.)

Week 28

1. **17.** Call the top point a, the points on the mid-line b and c, and those on the base d, e and f; then we have abc, (not abd – a straight line), abe, abf, acd, ace, (not acf), ade, adf, aef (8); bcd, bce, bcf, bde, bdf, bef (6); cde, cdf, cef (3); (not def). (Work systematically.)

2. **4 players refused to sign.** Using divisibility rules: 2607 = 3 × 11 × 79, so 11 (a majority) signed. (Work systematically.)

3. **4.5 and 13.5.** If we add the difference and the sum, we get double one of the numbers (try it with any two numbers); if we subtract the difference from the sum we get double the other. Alternatively, if the larger number is x, then
$$x + (x - 9) = 18$$
$$2x = 27$$
$$x = 13.5$$
(Guess and check; look for a pattern.)

4. **34 mm.** Looking at the books' spines, the first page is on the right of volume 1, while the last page is on the left of volume 3. Hence the distance is one book plus two covers. (Make a model.)

5. **6 × 7 × 8 × 9.** The numbers do not contain a multiple of 5, since the units digit is 4. 1 × 2 × 3 × 4 is too small. (Guess and check.)

Week 29

1. **4 leaves.** Page 8 is to the left when a standard book is open; the leaves are pages 9 and 10, 11 and 12, 13 and 14, and 15 and 16.

2. **There were 21 in the group.** In, say, a group of 4, each shakes 3 hands but it takes 2 hands for a shake so there are $4 \times 3 \div 2$ shakes. Hence we must find a number (n) whose product with ($n - 1$) is 210×2. (Make a simpler problem; guess and check; look for a pattern.)

3. Other solutions are where the coins form the faces of a tetrahedron. (Make a model.)

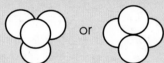

4. **17 children,** having 0, 1, 2 … 16 marbles each. If there were 18 children the number of marbles would be 0, 1, 2 … 16, 18 which is forbidden. The same holds for any larger number of children. (Make a simpler problem; look for a pattern.)

5. **61.** One less and the number is an exact mulitple of 4, 5 and 6. (See W 17/1).

Week 30

1. **Large plates $6, small plates $5.** The largest multiple of 17 below 100 is 85 = 17×5. There were thus 15 large plates to make up the remainder. Algebraically, with x, y, t the number of small plates and large plates and the cost in dollars of a small plate respectively:

$x + y = 17$

$xt + y(t + 1) = 100$,

so $xt + (17 - x)(t + 1) = 100$

$17t + 17 - x = 100$

$x = 17t - 83$

which is a Diophantine equation whose only solution, with x between 0 and 17, is $x = 2, t = 5$. Hence $y = 15$. (Guess and check; look for a pattern.)

2. **–5 and 15.** One number is half (the sum plus the difference); the other is half (the sum minus the difference). Algebraically, if the larger number is *x*, then

$x + (x – 20) = 10$.

(Guess and check; look for a pattern – see W28/3.)

3. **3 doughnuts!**

4.

5. **64.** Since any number has a unique set of prime factors, each factor occurs $2 \times 3 = 6$ times, the only such two-digit number is 2^6. (Work systematically.)

- -

Week 31

1. They are the numbers 1, 2, 3 … with each reflected in a 'vertical' mirror. (Different but similar answers are possible, since the mirror's position is not fixed.)

2. **35.** Call the edges in order *a, b, c, d, e, f, g*. There are 7 triangles with 2 sides on the heptagon (*abc, bcd, cde, def, efg, fga, gab*), 21 triangles with just 1 side on the heptagon (there are 7 edges and each has 3 triangles – *ab* has *abd, abe, abf*) and 7 triangles with no sides on the heptagon (*ace, bdf, ceg, dfa, egb, fac, gbd*). Althernatively, go round the heptagon in 3 jumps point to point in 5 different ways: (1, 1, 5), (1, 2, 4), (1, 3, 3), (1, 4, 2), (2, 2, 3) Starting at each point there are 7×5 triangles. (Work systematically.)

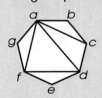

3. **10 hurdles.** There are no hurdles at the start or finish. (Draw a diagram.)

4. **2 × \$50, \$50 + (2 × \$20) + \$10, \$50 + \$20 + (3 × \$10), \$50 + (5 × \$10), 5 × \$20, (4 × \$20) + (2 × \$10), (3 × \$20) + (4 × \$10), (2 × \$20) + (6 × \$10), \$20 + (8 × \$10), 10 × \$10.** (Work systematically.)

5. **5 sheep and 25 ducks; 10 cows.** Algebraically, if *x, y* and *z* are the number of cows, sheep and ducks respectively,

$y + z = 3x$, and

$5y + 3z = 100$.

so $5y + 3(3x – y) = 100$

$2y + 9x = 100$.

Since *x* is thus even, the only solutions which make *y* and *z* both positive are (10, 5, 25) and (8, 14, 10). But there are a lot of ducks. (Guess and check; make a chart.)

Week 32

1. **A 6 with one die is more likely.** The chances are $\frac{1}{6}$ $(=\frac{6}{36})$, while the chances with 2 dice are $\frac{5}{36}$: (1,5), (2,4), (3,3), (4,2), (5,1).

2. **A = 9, F = 6, O = 1, X = 4.** $O^2 = O$, so $O = 1$; hence OF (a square number) = 16. $14^2 = 196$. (Use reasoning; see W1/5)

3. **You can expect to lose.** Assume you have $4 to start; a win followed by a loss gives $4 ➜ $6 ➜ $3 while a loss followed by a win gives $4 ➜ $2 ➜ $3. Either way you lose a quarter of your money for two different results in succession. In the long run, with about the same number of heads and tails, the situation will be repeated many times, and even a few extra wins will not save you! (Work systematically; make a chart.)

4.

5. **Alice should have 14 apples and Nancy 2 apples.** Since Karl gets 8 oranges for his 16 apples, an orange is worth 2 apples. Alice gives up 7 oranges and Nancy only 1 orange. (Use reasoning.)

Week 33

1. Generally speaking, n straight lines will form $\frac{n(n+1)}{2} + 1$ regions, so 3 lines make 7 regions, 4 make 11, 5 make 16 and so on. Beware! It is not always possible to go in reverse: for instance, 7 points on a circle cannot be isolated by 3 straight lines. (Look for a similar problem – see W 4/1.)

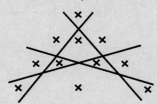

2. **11^{11} (= 285 311 670 611)**, since no signs are permitted, otherwise you could have $11!^{11^{11}}$ which is approximately 1 followed by more than 300,000,000 zeros!

3. **Chances are $\frac{15}{32}$ $(=\frac{5}{12})$.** Six pairs are the same, and 15 favour Flo. (Work systematically.)

4. **3 socks.** After a grey and a black the next will make up a pair. (Make a model.)

5. **The gold weighs 42 g.** The tin weighs 120 – 90 = 30 g and the bronze weighs 120 – 72 = 48 g. (Work systematically.)

Week 34

1. Each row and column adds to

$$\frac{3 + 4 + 5 + .. + 11}{3} = 21$$

8	3	10
9	7	5
4	11	6

and the middle number = 7. The rest follows. (Use reasoning; guess and check; look for a pattern.)

2. **Wanda is 12 and Yolande is 16.** By trial, Wanda is one of 3, 6, 9 etc. with Yolande 4, 8, 12 etc. In four years they will be 7 and 8, 10 and 12, or 13 and 16, or 16 and 20 – aha! Alternatively, if their ages at present are 3x and 4x years, then

    $3x + 4 = \frac{4}{5}(4x + 4)$
    $5(3x + 4) = 4(4x + 4)$
    $15x + 20 = 16x + 16$
    $x = 4$.
    (Make a chart.)

3. **3 ducks.** 2 ducks are behind the front duck, and 2 ducks are in front of the last duck.

4. **20 seconds.** The first car laps the second 3 times in a minute. (Use reasoning.)

5. **144 tiles.** Trial of the difference between two squares gives the result quite quickly. Using algebra, if x and y are the numbers after and before the extension, $(x + y)(x - y) = 80$. Both factors are even, giving 40×2, 20×4 and 10×8. Only 20 and 4 give x and y even; $x = 12$ and $y = 8$. (Form an equation.)

Week 35

1. **4% speak both languages.** 94 + 10 = 104, so 4% counts twice. (Use a Venn diagram.)

2. **Heke,** with Mickey second and Nikki third. Nikki did not win or come second (she was not the shortest). Heke must have won since he had a sister. (Use reasoning – see W1/2).

3. **The passenger train's speed was 90 km/h.** The lengths of the trains are quite irrelevant! If we make a chart showing the relative speeds of the passenger train in the same direction and in the opposite direction, we need just go on till one speed is double the other:

Actual speed	Rel. speed (same)	Rel. speed (opposite)
60 km/h	30 km/h	90 km/h
70 km/h	40 km/h	100 km/h
80 km/h	50 km/h	110 km/h
90 km/h	60 km/h	120 km/h

Algebraically, if v is the speed in km/h of the passenger train, then:

$(v + 30) = 2(v - 30)$
$2v - v = 30 + 60$
$v = 90$

(Guess and check; make a chart; look for a pattern.)

4.   103. You just have to take care!

5.   Australia 2–New Zealand 1, Australia 1–Fiji 0, New Zealand 3–Fiji 2.
Australia's scores must be 2–1 and 1–0, but if Fiji lost 1–2 to Australia their loss to
New Zealand would be 1–2 also, so New Zealand would have a 3–3 goal tally.
Hence Fiji lost 0–1 to Australia. (Use reasoning; work systematically; make a chart.)

Week 36

1.   Numerals at 20c a digit.

2.   C = 5, X = 7, I = 6. $I^2 = \_I$, so I = 0, 1, 5 or 6. I ≠ 0 or 5, since their squares would
not end in 00 or 25 (and 25^2 = 625 – a 3-digit number). Nor is I = 1, though this
argument is more subtle: comparing tens digits, X = 2 × X or X = 2 × X – 10, giving X
= 0 or 10 which cannot be solutions. Hence I = 6.
Again using the tens digit of each side,
12 × X + 3 = X + a multiple of 10,
i.e   11 × X = _7, so X = 7. 76^2 = 5776.
(It is probably quicker, and certainly easier, to do the second part by trial. Use
reasoning; work systematically – see W1/5)

3.   27 triangles.   Upright side 1:   10   Inverted side 1:   6
                        side 2:   6   Inverted side 2:   1
                        side 3:   3
                        side 4:   1
(Work systematically; make a simpler problem.)

4.

5.   8 litres. The volumes of similar figures are in the ratio of the cubes of the ratio of their
linear dimensions. This is most easily seen with two cubic shapes – eight 1 cm cubes
make a 2-cm cube. (Make a model.)

Week 37

1.   2 and 3, 1 and 6, 4 and 7, 5 and 9. Since the numbers total 37, the last card is
45 – 37 = 8. 14 must thus be 5 + 9, then 11 is 7 + 4, and 7 is 6 + 1. (Work
systematically.)

2.   7 cans of soft drink. The seventh is from recycling the six cans they drank
themselves. (Draw a diagram; act it out)

3.   22. Two colours might be exhausted before marbles are selected from the third. (Make
a model.)

4.

5. **The output from (2,3) is 12.** While there may be more complex relations, we would expect to try

$$1x + 2y = 7$$
$$2x + 1y = 8$$

which gives x = 3, y = 2. This is confirmed, since

$$1 \times 3 + 1 \times 2 = 5$$

and $\quad 2 \times 3 + 2 \times 2 = 10.$

(Form an equation; guess and check.)

Week 38

1. **5 Saturdays.** New Year's Day is also a Thursday, so there are Saturdays on the 3rd, 10th, 17th, 24th and 31st.

2. **4 socks.** To be sure of getting a pair, 3 socks are needed; so only 2 socks can be of the same colour. (Make a model; guess and check.)

3. **ABC = 248.** Since BCB has 3 digits, A is 1 or 2, but $A^2 \neq A$, so A = 2. $22^2 = 484$. (Use reasoning – see W1/5.)

4. **9 ways.** Let 'Ab' mean A has B's assignment:

If Ab, then Ba, Cd and Dc
or Bc, Cd and Da
or Bd, Ca and Dc.

Similarly, there are three ways with Ac and three ways with Ad. (Work systematically.)

5. **54 squares.** Each of the six faces has nine squares. (Make a model.)

Week 39

1. **6283 metres (about 6 km).** If the Earth's radius is R metres, the extra distance travelled in metres is $2\pi(R + 1000) - 2\pi R = 2000\pi$. (Draw a diagram.)

2. **First, place the 2-g weight on one pan, and balance to get 49 g + 2 g = 51 g. Second, weigh the 49 g of sawdust against the 2 g and restore the balance (49 g = 2 g + 47 g).** You will then have the required 47 g of sawdust. (Guess and check.)

3. **D = 1, O = 2, P = 8, R = 7.** $D^3 = D$, so D = 1. O can only be 0 or 2, or the cube would be more than 2000; since $10^3 = 1000$ which does not fit the required pattern, we have $12^3 = 1728$. (Use reasoning – see W1/5)

4. **The other was the mother.**

5. **40 points in every hundred.** When Avim gets 100, Adit should get 80; hence Adunof should get 60. The proportion of Adit giving 25% of the points is maintained. (Guess and check.)

Week 40

1. **She divides four cakes into twelve thirds and the other three into twelve quarters. Each child gets a quarter and a third.** (Draw a diagram.)

2. **12 days.** Since fine mornings and fine evenings make 15, and it rained on only 9 half-days, there must have been 15 – 9 = 6 half-days when the other half was also fine; that is, it was fine all of 3 days. There were 4 days when it was fine only in the morning and 5 days when it was fine only in the evening. (Guess and check; look for a pattern.)

3. **50.** We describe the sloping squares by the distances up and along the top left side (so the square shown is (1,2)). These components cannot add to more than four. We then have

(1,1)	$3 \times 3 = 9$
(1,2) and (2,1)	$2 \times 2 \times 2 = 8$
(1,3) and (3,1)	$2 \times 1 \times 1 = 2$
(2,2)	$1 \times 1 = 1$

   making 20. Then there are the 'level' squares

1 by 1	$4 \times 4 = 16$
2 by 2	$3 \times 3 = 9$
3 by 3	$2 \times 2 = 4$
4 by 4	$1 \times 1 = 1$

   (Work systematically; look for a pattern.)

4. **Barry wound up his clock, noted the time shown, walked to his friend's house, noted the correct time, stayed, noted the time as he left, walked back home, noted the apparent time since he had left home and subtracted from it the time he had stayed with his friend.** This gave his total walking time which he then halved, and finally corrected his clock to that amount forward of the time when he had left his friend's house.

5. **8 cubes.** If *r* represents a red side and *b* a blue side, they can be

1 r, 5 b (+ 5r, 1b)	2, (1 + 1)
2 r, 4 b (+ 4r, 2b)	4, (2 + 2)
3 r, 3 b	2

   For the 2, 4 pattern the 2 must be opposite or adjacent; for the 3, 3 pattern, either each colour consists of 3 mutually adjacent sides or both colours have a pair of opposite sides. (Make a model; work systematically.)

Holiday stretch answers

Autumn

1A. **The married couples are Bill and Nora, Charlie and Merle, and Don and Lucy.** Neither Bill nor Don is married to Merle; husbands and wives are not listed in the same order.

2A.

1	2	3	6
2	4	1	7
3	1	4	8
4	3	2	9

10 10 10

3A. **Otway is 5 km from Liston.** The triangle formed by Liston, Marfield and Newdle is right-angled at Liston, so Otway is the centre of the circle through them.

4A. **32 triangles can be formed.** There are 6 small equilateral triangles, 12 isosceles triangles with an angle of 120°, 12 right-angled triangles and 2 large equilateral triangles. (Alternatively, there are 35 ways of selecting 3 points from 7, 3 sets each forming a straight line.)

5A. **The proportions are the same** of course, since the volumes are equal. (If the original amounts were 6 units in each jar, the tea jar contains 6 units of tea and 3 of coffee after the first pour; 2 units of tea and 1 of coffee are then poured back, so the coffee jar contains 4 units of coffee and 2 of tea and vice versa for the tea jar.)

6A. **(a) C = 3, I = 6, L = 5, V = 0, (b) C = 2, I = 5, L = 4, V = 0.**
$I \times V = \_V$, so $V = 0$ or 5, or $I = 1$ or 6. If $V = 5$, I is odd; only $I = 1$ gives the correct tens digit in the product, but gives only 3 digits, so $V \neq 5$ (unless $L = 8$ which gives different values for C). If $I = 1$, $V \times L = \_0$, but $L \neq 0$ (initial digit) or 5 (3-digit product), and $V \neq 0$ (3-digit product). Hence $I \neq 1$. If $I = 6$, V is even and there is an even carry to the tens, so $V = 0$, 4 or 8. $V = 4$, 8 both fail, leaving $V = 0$, giving (a) $56 \times 60 = 3360$. If $I \neq 1$ or 6, $V = 0$ again and $I = 5$, giving (b) $45 \times 50 = 2250$.

7A. First weighing: weigh 200 g of sugar in a container against the 200 g weight and an empty container. Second weighing: split the 200 g of sugar into two containers till they balance. (Other solutions are possible.)

8A.

9A. **The smallest number is 186.** Take the numbers with a remainder of 6 when divided by 9: 15, 24, 33 ... till you get a remainder of 4 on division by 7. This gives 60 and hence also 60 + any multiple of $9 \times 7 = 63$. Continue till you get 2 more than a multiple of 4.

10A. **The piles have 5, 7, 8 and 25 marbles.** $7000 = 2^3 \times 5^3 \times 7$ and since the sum is 9×5, exactly 2 factors are multiples of 5 and 2 are not. The sum of the latter factors must also be a multiple of 5. The only possibilities are 1 and 4, 1 and 14, 2 and 28 or 7 and 8. Only the last pair gives a total of 45.

Winter

1W. (The two columns are interchangeable.)

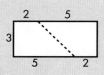

2W.

3W. **The steady car wins by 400 m.** 2 km at 50 km/h takes 2.4 minutes. 1 km at 30 km/h takes 2 minutes, and the first car descends for 0.4 minutes at 90 km/h, travelling just 600 m.

4W. **There can be 8 regions for 4 points, 16 regions for 5 points and 31 regions for 6 points.** Although 1 point gives 1 region, 2 points give 2 regions, 3 points give 4 regions, 4 points give 8 regions and 5 points give 16 regions; the pattern is not a doubling one. There is a pattern, however, obtained by taking differences of successive terms:

```
1       2       4       8       16       (31)       (57) ...
    1       2       4       8       (15)       (26) ...
        1       2       4       (7)       (11) ...
            1       2       (3)       (4) ...
```

You can check that there are 57 regions possible with 7 points (draw a large circle!).

5W.

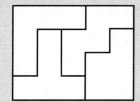

6W. **GO = 82, STOP = 6724.** O $\neq$ 1, 5 or 6 since O $\neq$ P; nor is O = 3, 7 or 9 which make the tens digit in the product even, while O = 4 makes it odd. If O = 8, G = 2 gives a 3-digit product, while G = 7 gives 6084 with T being zero. Hence O = 2 and G = 8, since G = 3 also has T being zero in the product (1024).

7W. **Alex was the teacher** (obviously!)

8W. **The hands were last together at 10.54 $\frac{6}{11}$ a.m**. Since the minute hand travels at twelve times the hour hand, they meet every $\frac{1}{11}$ of a revolution of the hour hand, or 1 hour and 5 $\frac{5}{11}$ minutes.

9W. **The smallest number is 367.** Take the sequence 15, 26, 37 ... till you get a remainder of 3 on division by 7; this is 59. Now add multiples of 7 × 11 = 77 (to keep these two remainders the same) for the desired result.

10W. $a = 9$, $b = 5$, $c = 2$. If we consider multiples of 3, 5 and 7 in turn, we can write:

$3(5a + 7b + 11c) + 2c = 3 \times 103 + 1$

$5(3a + 4b + 7c) + b = 5 \times 62$

$7(2a + 3b + 5c) + a = 7 \times 44 + 2$

Hence a is from 2, 9, 16 ..., b is from 5, 10, 15 ... and c is from 2, 5, 8 ... If $a = 2$, the equation boils down to $3b + 5c = 40$ whose solution gives repeated values. If $a = 16$ we get $3b + 5c = 10$ (no solution), and similarly for larger values of a. Hence $a = 9$ and $3b + 5c = 25$.

Spring

1P. **There were 200 people in the hall.** 11% were male graduates, so 44% were female graduates. Women who were not graduates (just 2 people) thus formed 100% – 55% – 44% = 1% of those at the meeting.

2P.

1	2	3	5	11
3	5	1	2	11
5	3	2	1	11
2	1	5	3	11
11	11	11	11	

3P. **Neddie bought 17 stamps at 35c and 9 stamps at 45c.** If he bought x stamps at 35c and y stamps at 45c, then

$$35x + 45y = 1000$$

i.e. $7x + 9y = 200$

Now subtract 7s from 200 till you get a multiple of 9: 56 + 144; since these are even, subtract a further $7 \times 9 = 63$, giving 119 + 81.

4P. **The radius is 20 cm.** In the diagram below $OA = 10$ cm and $\angle AOB = 60°$, so triangle OAB is half an equilateral triangle. Hence $OB = 2 \times OA$.

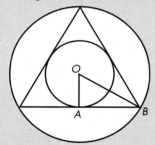

5P. **You can have \$4.35.** The coins are $1 \times \$2$, $1 \times \$1$, $1 \times 50c$, $4 \times 20c$ and $1 \times 5c$.

6P.

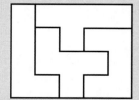

7P. **The numbers are 1, 4 and 21.** $84 = 2^2 \times 3 \times 7$ and 2 of the numbers must be odd to get an even sum. 3 and 7 don't work, so 1 must be used.

8P. **Abi was a Pert, Ebi a Zert and Ubi a Quert.** Ebi is not a Pert since she states that Ubi is; Ubi is not a Pert since her statements would then be contadictory.

9P. **I = 4, V = 8, X = 1.** If I = 1 or 2 the sum has only 2 digits. If I = 3, V = 1, also giving 2 digits. I ≠ 5 which gives V also 5. None of the larger values for I give a correct tens digit in the sum, so I = 4 and V = 8.

10P. **There are 80 different oblongs.**
With sides parallel to the sides of the square:

2 by 1 ➝	12	3 by 2 ➝ 6	
3 by 1 ➝	8	4 by 2 ➝ 3	
4 by 1 ➝	4	4 by 3 ➝ 2	
1 by 2 ➝	12	2 by 3 ➝ 6	
1 by 3 ➝	8	2 by 4 ➝ 3	
1 by 4 ➝	4	3 by 4 ➝ 2	

(total 70)
with sides parallel to the main diagonals:

2 by 1 ➝	4	1 by 2 ➝ 4	
3 by 1 ➝	1	1 by 3 ➝ 1	

(total 10).

Summer

1U.

6	7	8	9	30
3	4	5	2	14
4	1	2	5	12
2	5	3	1	11
17	15	17	18	17 13

2U. **Carol broke the window.** Just one of Billy and Carol told the truth, so Archie was lying.

3U. **The clock and watch gave the same times on 25 May and 16 October 2005.** Each day there is a further difference of 5 minutes between them, so it will take $12 \times 12 = 144$ days to give the same time.

4U. **There are 28 different triangles.** There are 18 triangles of base 1 unit, 4 upright and 4 inverted triangles of base 2 units and two with base 3 units.

5U. **Aim at C.**

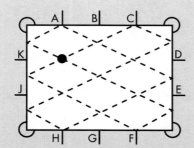

6U. **The stamp values are 40c and 20c respectively.** There are 100 units of 5c in $5; keep subtracting 11 from 100 till you are left with a multiple of 7. This gives 100 − 44 = 56, i.e. $7 \times 8 + 11 \times 4 = 100$, so the values are 8 units and 4 units.

7U.

23	5	11
1	13	25
15	21	3

or its reflection in the leading diagonal.

8U. **The cuboid is 20 cm by 3 cm by 2 cm.** If the sides are a, b and c cm long, then the total side length is $4a + 4b + 4c$, so $abc = 120$ and $a + b + c = 25$. Since $120 = 2^3 \times 3 \times 5$ and the sum is odd, just one of a, b, c is odd.

9U.

10U. **(Home team first) Farrar drew with Exington and beat Dorham; Exington beat Farrar and drew with Dorham; Dorham lost to Farrar but beat Exington.**

Since 15 points were scored, 3 games were home wins (2 points each) and 3 other results (3 points each). Neither Farrar nor Dorham had 2 draws since Farrar had only 2 home games and Dorham's results (2 away draws, 2 home losses) would leave only 2 home wins. Hence Exington drew with Farrar (away) and Dorham (home), and all three sides had one home win; Farrar's away win was against Dorham.

Benders

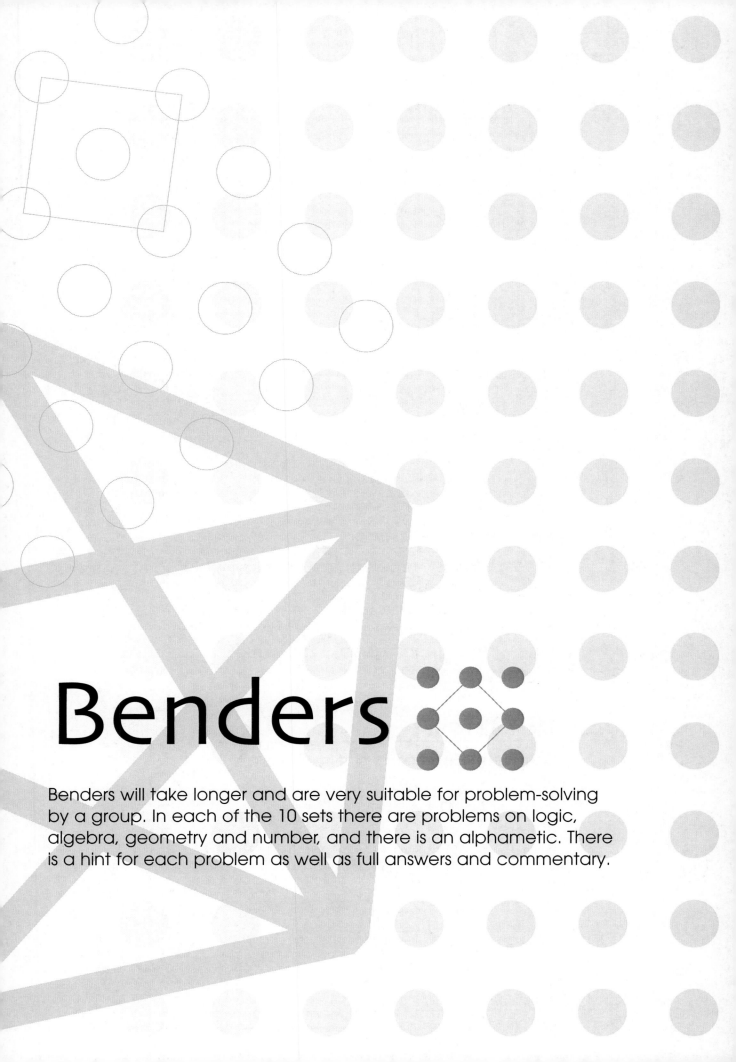

Benders will take longer and are very suitable for problem-solving by a group. In each of the 10 sets there are problems on logic, algebra, geometry and number, and there is an alphametic. There is a hint for each problem as well as full answers and commentary.

1a.   My first alphametic

In alphametic problems where letters stand for numbers, each letter represents a different digit and numbers do not begin with the digit 0. What do the letters stand for?

```
    ABCD
+   ADAC
    BCDC
```

1b.   The swimming pool

Jack and Jill had a swimming race of two lengths of the pool. Jack started at the west end and passed Jill (who started at the east end) 7 metres from his end the first time and 6 metres from her end the second time. Assuming each swam steadily with no time for the turnaround, who won and by what distance?

1c.   Relatively interesting

In her sociology report on a community, Margaret stated:
• There were more parents than children
• Every girl had a brother
• There were more girls than boys.
Why was her report given a fail grade?

1d.   The Taj Mahal

Each letter represents a different digit.
Solve:

```
          B O Y
  I N ) D I A N
        T Y
        Y Y A
        Y A T
          I N
          I N
```

1e.   Watch the clock

Shortly after noon, Nadia went to lunch. On
her return the hour and the minute hand had
changed places. How long was she
away?

1f.   3 out of 8

How many different triangles can be
formed whose vertices are the corners
of a regular octagon?

1g.   Not quite Wimbledon

In the tennis league each match is the best of 11 games.
The final table, with each team playing the others once,
was:

	Won	Lost	For	Against
Cardinals	2	1	23	10
Blues	2	1	18	15
Kiwis	1	2	13	20
Ockers	1	2	12	21

If the Kiwis beat the Blues 8–3 but were annihilated by the
Cardinals, and all scores were different, what were they?

1h.   They won't eat you

On the island of Om there were three missionaries and
three cannibals who needed to cross the River Chops. They
had a boat which could take two people. In order not to
risk being eaten, the missionaries had to ensure that they
were never outnumbered on either bank.
What was the smallest number of crossings possible to ferry
all six?

2a. A little backward

Can you find a four-figure number which is reversed when multiplied by nine?

2b. The lost emperor

When the digits from this puzzle are put in order from 0 to 9 the letters form a keyword. What is it?

```
            N H S A
  N O )C H A R T
        R N
        O R A
        O N H
          O I R
          O H S
            H T
            H A
              H
```

2c. Hair today, gone tomorrow

Maria, Alison and Carol were a blonde, a brunette and a redhead. While out shopping, Carol spent twice as much as Alison who spent three times as much as Maria.
If the blonde spent $7.25 more than the redhead, what colour hair did each have and how much did they each spend?

2d. Nine over two

Divide the nine squares into two equal areas with a straight line through *A*.

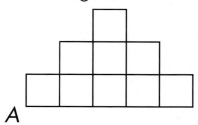

2e.   What are four fives?

Using the numeral 5 four times in each, make up equations for the numbers from 1 to 10. (You may use any arithmetic symbols needed.)

2f.   A staffing problem

Anne, Barbara and Donna are in the purchasing, marketing and sales departments. The woman in sales, who earns the most, is an only child. Anne, who married Barbara's brother, earns less than the woman in marketing. Who is in which department?

2g.   Can you count the alphabet?

Each letter in the following stands for a different digit.
What does each represent?

$$
\begin{array}{r}
A\ A\ A \\
+\ B\ B\ B \\
\hline
C\ C\ C\ D
\end{array}
\qquad
A\,\overline{)\,C\ C\ C\ D}\ ^{A\ B\ D}
$$

2h.   In the teacups

Half the people at the tea table do not take sugar, a quarter do not take milk, a third take milk and sugar, and two take neither.
How many are there at the tea table?

3a. The carpenter's square

A carpenter has a symmetrical piece of wood whose shape is formed by a square and a right-angled triangle. With just two straight cuts he is able to make three pieces which can then be moved to form a perfect square.
How?

3b. Lots of *Ludo*

Three friends, Pete, Pat and Pet, played six games of *Ludo*. The order was different every time, but I noticed that no-one who came first in one game was last in the next, and no-one who was last in one game came first in the next.
If Pete won the first two games and Pet won the third, what were the exact placings in each game?

3c. Exhibition time

At a mathematics exhibition there were 250 entries from 13 schools. If the largest number of entries from a school is x, what is the smallest possible value for x?

3d. A musical problem

Find the different digit represented by each letter (each letter represents a different digit).

$$\begin{array}{r} T\,O\,O\,T \\ \times \qquad A \\ \hline N\,O\,T\,E \end{array}$$

3e.   The new stations

Every station on the railway sells tickets for every other station. When the line was extended with new stations, an extra 46 tickets had to be printed.
How many new stations were there?

3f.   See the buses

A bus leaves the city, and other buses coming in the opposite direction at the same speed pass it once every 10 minutes.
How many buses an hour come into the city by that route?

3g.   Friends in the store

In a department store the positions of buyer, cashier, clerk, floorwalker and manager are held by Miss Ang, Miss Bundy, Mr Casey, Mr Dupont and Mr Evans.
The buyer is a bachelor, and the cashier and manager were room-mates at university. Mr Evans and Miss Ang had only business contacts with each other, Mrs Casey was disappointed when the manager refused her husband a raise, and Mr Dupont is going to be best man when the clerk marries the cashier.
What position does each person hold?

3h.   A musical card game

A pack of cards for Bridge has two red suits and two black suits, each of 13 cards. When the Singhs played the Cheungs recently, the number of red cards held by the Singhs exceeded that of their opponents by the number of black cards held by Mr Cheung (who also held the two red aces).
If Mr Singh held twice as many black cards as Mr Cheung held red cards, how many red and black cards did each player hold?

4a. The footpath

On a square plot of land of 21 metres each side, an angled strip of 21 m² is dedicated to a footpath.
How long is the path *AB*?

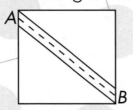

4b. A funny answer

When the numbers 0 to 9 are placed in order, the letters which represent them make a keyword.
What is it?

```
   R T I R S H I H E
 + E T E R A H R I R
 ─────────────────
   L C Y Y H Y Y I L
```

4c. Across the desert

An explorer is planning a trip across a desert which will take six days. He can only carry 4 full water bottles at a time.
If he needs to drink 1 full bottle each day to survive, how long must he take to cross the desert (including the time required to return for more water)?

4d. The hungry cows

In a field where the grass grows at a steady rate, 40 cows can last 20 days, or 30 cows can last 30 days.
How long would 25 cows last?

4e. Stealing sheep

Each letter represents a different digit.
What does each letter stand for?

```
          V E
D I ) V I D E
    F E E
    E W E
    T I E
      U P
```

4f. Candles in a jar

Two candles 20 cm high are each in a jar, with one jar having twice the depth of the other. The top of the first candle was half as much above the top of the smaller jar as the top of the second candle was below the top of the larger jar.
How deep was each jar?

4g. Questionable characters

On the island of Qua no-one ever makes a statement, they only ask questions. There are two types of people – the Yeah who always ask questions with the answer 'Yes', and the Neah who always ask questions with the answer 'No'. Even with these weird people it is possible to gain some information. What can you conclude from the following about the type of people involved?

(i) Gordon asked his wife Eleanor 'Are we different?'

(ii) Rehto asked 'Am I the type who could ask this question?'

4h. How many points in a triangle?

Can you put five distinct points inside an equilateral triangle of side 2 units so that the closest two are more than 1 unit apart?

5a. The old wreck

Each letter represents a different digit. Find each digit:

```
   L I S T
 - S I L T
 ─────────
   S L I T
```

5b. Where is the silver cross?

In Transylvania, there are humans and
vampires. Humans tell the truth if sane but
lie if insane, while vampires lie if sane
but tell the truth if insane. The
Radevich brothers, one of whom
was known to be a vampire while
the other was human, made the
following statements:

Boris: I am human.
Carlo: I am human.
Boris: My brother is sane.
What can you say about the brothers?

5c. Easy as A, B, C

Write down the set of letters A, B, C in each of its six possible
orders so that when all 18 letters are written around a circle,
adjacent letters are always different.

5d. Keep to the subject

At the Student Council each subject had four
representatives, each student represented two subjects,
and every pair of subjects had one representative in
common.
How many subjects were represented?

5e. We are broke

Find the digit represented by each letter.
A letter can stand for only one digit.

```
    S E N D
  + M O R E
  ---------
  M O N E Y
```

5f. Look at the table

It was an incredible season in the Junior Soccer League, with goals galore. Although the scores were different in each of the six matches, the total of goals per match was always the same. The final table, with 2 points for a win and 1 point for a draw, was:

	Goals for	Goals against	Points
Kaimana	13	17	4
Barham	17	13	3
Potridge	17	13	3
Sapford	13	17	2

If Sapford scored 2 goals against Potridge, what were the scores?

5g.   To get to the other side

Two adults and a girl arrive with a suitcase at a river where a boy runs a ferry.

How can they all get across and the ferry returned if it will only take one adult, or two children, or the boy and the suitcase?

5h.   Two squares in one

Using just 2 straight cuts on a square of side 4 units, place the pieces together with a unit square to form a single square.

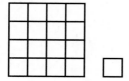

6a.   Biological multiplication

Each digit represents a different letter, H being odd.
Find the digit each letter stands for.

```
      O N E
  ×   O N E
  ─────────
  T H R E E
```

6b.   Andy's taps

While experimenting with the taps that fill a vat, Andy discovered that the vat would fill in 5 hours if four red taps and three black taps were on, but it took only 4 hours if four red taps and five black taps were on.
How long would it have taken if he had turned on four red taps and four black taps?

6c.   The roadside stall

Kiwifruit are five for $1, apples are four for $1 and pears are three for $1. Peter, Bonny and Don each get 20 pieces of fruit for $5.
What were their selections if Peter had the most kiwifruit and Bonny had the most apples?

6d.   The hidden sum

Manu wrote his homework in code, but his addition was correct.
What was the code?

```
    5 8 9 2
  + 5 2 8 9
  ─────────
    8 9 5 9
```

6e.   They own the village

The Smith family, which consists of Mr and Mrs Smith, their son Alan, Mrs Smith's father and Mrs Smith's sister Gwen, has for years dominated the community life of Te Rama. At the present time the five members of their family hold the positions of grocer, lawyer, postmaster, teacher and minister in the village.

The lawyer and the teacher are not blood relatives; the grocer is younger than her sister-in-law but older than the teacher, while the minister (who played rugby for his school) is older than the postmaster.

What position did each member of the family hold?

6f.   The beach balls

Two beach balls of 140 cm and 60 cm diameter are on level ground and touching.
How high above the ground is their contact point?

6g.   A barter starter

In Woland, 2 clubs are worth 3 fishhooks and a lamp, and 50 yams will purchase 3 clubs, 2 lamps and a fishhook.
How many (whole) yams are needed for each of a club, a lamp and a fishhook?

6h.   Large letters – small number

If A, B and C represent different digits, what is the smallest possible value of the fraction?

$$\frac{ABC}{A + B + C}$$

7a.   Pythagoras regained

A constructive 'proof' of Pythagoras's theorem goes as follows: The square at *A* and the four pieces making up the square at *B* can be put together to make a square on side *C*.

Can you draw the right lines on *B* then rearrange the pieces to form the square on side *C*?

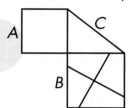

7b.   Dee dah dee dah

Morse code is made up of combinations of dots and dashes with a maximum of four symbols for any letter of the alphabet.

How many possible combinations are there?

Can you find those which are not used for any letter?

7c.   Go for the basket

The basketball league decided it needed to give credit to teams which won by large margins, so it decided on the following scoring system:

10 points or more difference:

Winners 12 points, losers 0 points

Less than 10 difference:

Winners 7 points, losers 4 points

Tie:

Each side 5 points

After playing each of the other sides just once, the points table was:

Cardinals   29
Polygons   24
Hyperbolas 11
Rationals   4

What were the results of the six games?

7d. Trial by daffodil

Mrs Tulip bought a daffodil for each year of her age next birthday. Unfortunately she dropped half of them, her grandchildren 'borrowed' a third of those that were left for a game, and 21 others had wilted before her birthday. Which birthday was it if she had just one daffodil left?

7e. Bingo!

LO + TTO = LOT.
What digit does each letter stand for?

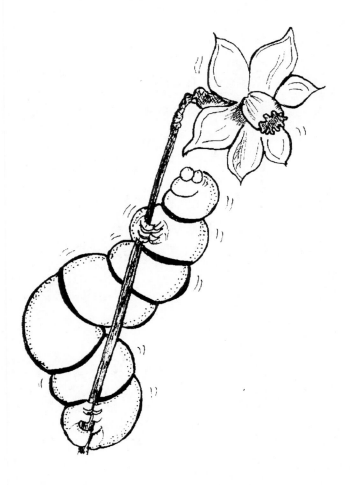

7f.   The hidden message

The grid of lines in the diagram shows a set of corridors. A secret message has been hidden at one of the intersections and the security agent has been tipped off that the spy has been told to start at the north-west corner and to travel only south or east. Furthermore, she knew that the spy had not been told directly which intersection to find, but only that there were 56 ways to get there. That was enough for the agent who then caught the spy at the intersection and so found the secret message as well.

Where was it?

```
        A   B   C   D   E   F   G   H
    a
    b
    c
    d
    e
```

7g.   Perfect match

Find the different digit represented by each letter.

```
              T O
    M A ) R R Y
          Y M
        ─────
        B O Y
        B A A
        ─────
          M T
```

7h. Hockey havoc

There are five hockey teams in the league. In the middle of the first round, part of the table was as follows.

	Played	Won	Lost	Drawn	Goals for	Goals against
A	3			1	4	2
B	1				2	1
C		0		0	3	4
D				1	3	2
E						

Find the score in each match played.

8a. All at sixes and sevens

Find a five-digit number with the property that a 1 placed behind it makes it three times as large as it is with a 1 before it.

8b. The hungry student

Each letter stands for a different digit. Which?

$$
\begin{array}{r}
\text{M E A L} \\
\times \quad\quad\quad \text{A} \\
\hline
\text{T E R M}
\end{array}
$$

8c. The domino theory

In a game of Dominoes there are 28 dominoes going from 0–0 to 6–6. Any domino can start in the version played but each new domino must have a number to match one end of the chain already formed.
(For example if the chain were 3–6, 6–2, 2–4, the new domino must have a 3 or 4 on one half.)
For the first two rounds Anna played dominoes totalling 23, Bella's totalled 20, Cara's 18 and Dana's 16. If they played in the order shown here and Dana did not play 6–2, who played which dominoes in what order?

8d. The round table

A circular table is pushed into a corner so that its edge is touching both walls. A spot on the edge is 18 cm from one wall and 25 cm from the other.
Find the diameter of the table.

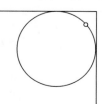

8e.   Don't feed the tigers!

Seven prisoners (A to G) are seated in order clockwise around a table. The guard said 'You are to pass the parcel to the prisoner on your left. The ninth person will be fed to the tigers and this activity will continue in the same way until there is only one prisoner left. He, thanks to the mercy of the Great One, will be let free.' D was actually in the pay of the Great One. Who should receive the parcel from the guard to make sure D is freed?

8f.   The modern alarm

Each letter in the puzzle below represents a digit from 0 to 9. If the digits 0 to 9 are placed in order, the letters representing them form a keyword. What is it?

```
        D O O R
    ×     R A Y
    ─────────────
        D O O R
    Y O A M I H
    T R D C H H
    ─────────────
    I I Y C D R
```

8g.   Starlings on a tree

At the 'starling ritual' seven starlings arrive at the tree to join those already there, then half the starlings fly away. This happens seven times over, after which there are just eight starlings left on the tree.
How many starlings were on the tree originally?

8h.   The plots thicken

Peter and his sister Polly were each given a rectangular block of land. Each block had sides of an exact number of metres, and the diagonals of each measured exactly 100 metres, yet Polly's block was almost twice as large as Peter's.
What were the dimensions of each block?

9a.   A change of tune

Each letter in this puzzle represents a digit from 0 to 9. If the digits 0 to 9 are placed in order, the letters representing them form a keyword.
What is it?

```
      A L T E R
  ×     N O T E
      A L T E R
    U G I T T R
    L U T O O R
    L N E L N R
  A U O A R N G E R
```

9b.   Hobbies

Mary, Alan and Rana are a scientist, a linguist and a spy and they collect stamps, coins and butterflies. Mary lives between the spy and the lepidopterist. Rana does not like the spy, while Alan and the numismatist are related.
Who has which hobby?

9c.   A balancing act

If two cylinders balance three cones and a cube, and five cones balance two cylinders and two cubes, how many cylinders and cones are needed to balance 10 cubes?

9d.   Coloured triangles

Five points are joined in pairs by either a blue line or a red line, with each point joined to every other point.
Can this be done without forming a red triangle or a blue triangle?
What about six points?

9e.   We don't get change

At the post office Eric handed over a pile of 10-cent pieces and asked for 45-cent and 80-cent stamps to their value. The assistant was most apologetic and stated 'I'm afraid that's impossible; if you can give me one or more extra 10-cent pieces, I can guarantee to meet your request however many you get.'
How much had Eric handed over?

9f.   The know-all neighbour

A neighbour made the following statements about Mr and Mrs Robbie and their two children:
>   Peter and Gwen are blood relatives.
>   Harry is older than Peter.
>   Sally is younger than Harry.
>   Sally is older than Gwen.
Only two of these statements turned out to be true. Who's who?

9g.   Two kinds of partner

Four married couples play mixed doubles at tennis together regularly, but the spouses are never partners. Find:
(i) the number of ways in which four pairings can be made
(ii) the number of possible matches.

9h.   The Romans were close

If each letter represents a different digit, find M, C and I.

$$
\begin{array}{r}
C\ C\ I \\
+\ C\ M\ I \\
\hline
M\ C\ C
\end{array}
$$

10a. Arrange the counters

Arrange nine counters on a flat surface so that there are 10 rows, each with three counters.

10b. Broken time

My clock has Roman numerals with cracks on its face. I noticed that the cracks divided the clock into four parts, each of which had the same total. Show how this could happen.

10c. Eggsactly

My farm eggs are boxed in 20s. Each week I get the same number of full boxes and loose eggs (a few more than 20). After six weeks I noticed that I had received the same number of boxes as I bought loose eggs each week, and the same number of loose eggs, after boxing sets of 20, as I bought boxes each week.
What is my weekly supply?

10d. Love games

Ed, Frank, George and Henry went with their wives to play tennis. Betty and Ed, Alice and Carol's husband, Dorothy and Alice's husband, Frank and George's wife, and George and Ed's wife were all partners.
Who were the husband and (different) partner of each woman?

10e.   Square the cross

A Greek cross consists of five equal squares. The problem is to cut it into four identical parts which can be rearranged to form a square.

10f.   Advice to a gambler

Each letter represents a different digit.
Which letter stands for which digit?

```
      B E T
   ×    O N
  ---------
    T E N
    B E T
  ---------
  T H A T
```

10g.   Four fields

Two adjoining rectangular fields have a common boundary. The sides of one field are 30 metres and 50 metres greater than the sides of the other, and it has twice the area.
Find their dimensions if there is a smaller pair of fields with exactly the same attributes.

10h.   Black or white?

Three people are blindfolded and each has either a white dot or a black dot glued to their forehead. They are told that not all the dots are black, and they must guess the colour of their own dot. The blindfolds are all simultaneously removed; after a long pause one said, 'My dot is white.' How did she know?

Hints for Benders

Section 1

a. $C + A = 10$

b. The distances travelled are proportional to the (constant) speeds.

c. Find the smallest possible number of children altogether.

d. Find Y first; $IN \times B = TY$

e. The minute hand had travelled about an hour at 12 times the speed of the hour hand.

f. Find the number of ways in which each corner can be chosen.

g. Find all the Blues' scores.

h. The missionaries are safe in the boat. Experiment.

Section 2

a. $9 \times 1 = 9$.

b. Look at each multiplication; why must O be 1 or 6?

c. Find the factors of 725.

d. Use the area of a right-angled triangle.

e. You can use .5.

f. Go for the woman in sales.

g. $C = 1$; find $A + B$.

h. Sugar + milk − both + neither = all.

Section 3

a. If the given square has an area of 4 square units, the required square has an area of 5 square units.

b. Experiment.

c. If x is smaller the others are larger.

d. $A \times T \leq N$; try out the possible values of T.

e. Each of *n* stations requires (n − 1) tickets.

f. What happens after half an hour?

g. Find out about Mr Dupont.

h. Red cards and black cards in any hand total 13; there are 26 red cards altogether.

Section 4

a. Find the area of each right-angled triangle.

b. Consider $R + E$ and the tens column.

c. It takes two water bottles to go one day's journey and back; drop off as needed.

d. If a cow eats 1 unit of grass each day, how fast must the grass grow each day?

e. I × E and I × V both end in E.

f. Let the jars be x and $2x$ cm high.

g. Experiment.

h. Draw in the unit triangles.

Section 5

a. Start with the ones, then the hundreds.

b. Experiment.

c. Experiment.

d. If there are n subjects, how many pairs contain a particular subject?

e. Go for the thousands.

f. Find the number of goals scored in each match. There was only one draw.

g. Experiment.

h. Find the required area; the cut pieces are identical.

Section 6

a. $E = 0$; $O \times O \leq T$.

b. How much of a vat does a red tap or a blue tap fill in an hour?

c. Experiment.

d. Go for the ones and the hundreds.

e. Who are Alan's relatives?

f. Use similar triangles.

g. Count in yams, put out the lamp and remember Diophantus.

h. A is small.

Section 7

a. The square's side must have the same length as the hypotenuse.

b. Each combination of dots and dashes has 1, 2, 3 or 4 symbols.

c. How could each team get its points?

d. Work backwards.

e. Start with the hundreds, then experiment with the ones and tens.

f. Find the number of routes from each intersection (starting at the north-west corner) and look for a pattern.

g. The only distinct digits whose product ends in 1 are 3 and 7. Is M equal to 1?

h. C lost – to whom?

Section 8

a. Moving the number one place to the left multiplies it by ten.

b. $A \times M \leq T$. Experiment with M.

c. Find the possible dominoes played by each; experiment.

d. Use Pythagoras from the centre of the table.

e. Experiment.

f. $R \times D \leq T$. Experiment with R.

g. Work backwards.

h. A multiple of 4 is only the sum of two perfect squares if they are even.

Section 9

a. Find E and R. Use the tens multiplier; when does $T \times T$ end in T?

b. A lepidopterist collects butterflies, a numismatist coins; who is the spy?

c. Use cubes as your unit.

d. Consider the lines from one point.

e. Experiment with sequences (e.g. $8 \times 5 + 9 \times 0 = 40$, $8 \times 4 + 9 \times 1 = 41$, $8 \times 3 + 9 \times 2 = 42$ …).

f. What happens if the second statement is true? Experiment.

g. Experiment.

h. Go for M in the tens.

Section 10

a. Experiment in sets of three.

b. Break up the IX.

c. Get the expressions for full boxes and loose eggs.

d. Go for Ed's wife.

e. The required square has an area of 5 unit squares.

f. 3 and 7 are the only distinct digits whose product ends in 1.

g. The longest side has twice the length of the shortest.

h. What are the others thinking?

Benders answers

1a. **A = 3, B = 6, C = 7, D = 0.** From the units, D = 0 and from the tens C + A = 10. From the hundreds, B = C − 1, since C ≠ 0, and from the thousands 2 × A = B. Putting A and B in terms of C,

$2 \times (10 - C) = C - 1$

$3 \times C = 21$

The result follows: 3670 + 3037 = 6707.

1b. **Jill won by 3.75 metres.** They swam 1 length between them at the first meeting and 3 lengths between them at the second meeting; hence the time to the second meeting is 3 times that to the first.

Jack has swum 7 m at the first meeting

and   pool's length + 6 m at second meeting

so   pool's length in metres + 6 = 3 × 7.

The pool is 15 m long, Jill travelled 15 − 7 = 8 m while Jack travelled 7 m, and when Jill had travelled the full 30 m, Jack had gone $\frac{7}{8} \times 30$ = 26.25m.

Algebraically, if Jill has travelled x metres when they meet for the first time, the pool must be $(x + 7)$ metres long, and so Jill will have travelled $(x + 1)$ metres on the second length when they pass again. Hence Jill has travelled x metres when Jack has gone 7 metres, and a total of $(7 + x) + (x + 1)$ metres when Jack has gone $(7 + x) + 6$ metres. So

$\frac{x}{7} = \frac{2x+8}{x+13}$

$x^2 + 13x = 14x + 56$

$x^2 - x - 56 = 0$

$(x - 8)(x + 7) = 0$

and x is 8 metres (discarding the meaningless negative solution).

1c. **The first statement must be false if the other two are true.**

If a is the number of families with one child (a boy)

     b is the number of families with 2 children (boy & girl or 2 boys)

     c is the number of families with more than 2 children (at least 1 boy),

     d is the total number of children,

then number of parents $\leq 2(a + b + c)$;

     number of boys $\geq a + b + c$;

     number of girls $\leq d - (a + b + c)$.

so $(a + b + c) \leq d - (a + b + c)$,

    $2(a + b + c) \leq d$

and there were thus at least as many children as parents.

1d. **A = 0, B = 3, D = 9, I = 2, N = 7, O = 4, T = 8, Y = 1.**

IN × Y = IN, Y = 1 and I − Y = Y, so I = 2.

Since 2N × B = T1 (a two digit number), B = 3 and N = 7, so T = 8.

YAT < YYA, so A = 0 and YAT is thus 108 (= 4 × 27) with O = 4.

D = T + Y, so D = 9. 9207 ÷ 27 = 341.

1e. $55\frac{5}{13}$ **minutes.** If the hour hand before lunch is at x minute divisions and the minute hand thus at $12x$ minute divisions (it moves 60 divisions while the hour hand moves 5), then after lunch the minute hand will be at x minute divisions and the hour hand at $12x$ minute divisions – this is obviously after 1 o'clock. Hence 60 + x (hour hand) = 12(12x) (minute hand), and $x = \frac{60}{143}$. The minute hand had travelled round from $\frac{720}{143}$ or $5\frac{5}{143}$ divisions, i.e. a distance of 60 − $\frac{660}{143}$ divisions.

1f.   **56 triangles.** The first vertex can be chosen in eight ways, the second in seven ways and the third in six ways. In this way each triangle is counted six times (*ABC, ACB, BAC, BCA, CAB, CBA*), so the number of ways is $(8 \times 7 \times 6) \div 6$.

1g.   **Cardinals: 2–9 v. Blues, 10–1 v. Kiwis, 11–0 v. Ockers;**
Blues: 3–8 v. Kiwis, 6–5 v. Ockers;
Kiwis: 4–7 v. Ockers.
Without the given result, Blues had a 15–7 goal tally for 2 wins and Kiwis had a 5–17 goal tally for 2 losses. Blues' other results must be 6–5 and 9–2; Kiwis' other results must therefore be 4–7 and 1–10. Hence Cardinals must have beaten Ockers 11–0 (the only other combination) and Kiwis 10–1 (annihilation), losing to Blues 2–9.

1h.   **6 over and 5 back.**

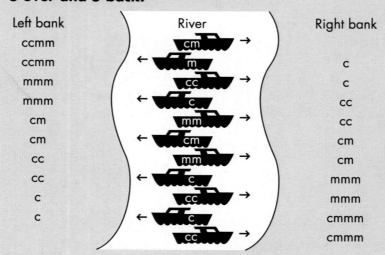

Left bank	River	Right bank
ccmm	cm →	
ccmm	← m	c
mmm	cc →	c
mmm	← c	cc
cm	mm →	cc
cm	← cm	cm
cc	mm →	cm
cc	← c	mmm
c	cc →	mmm
c	← c	cmmm
	cc →	cmmm

2a.   **1089.** The first digit must be 1 and the last 9 to keep the multiple to four digits. Also the digit sum is a multiple of 9 since 9 is a factor of the reversed number. Since the second digit is 0 or 1 (again to retain four digits) and 1179×9 is too large, 1089 is the only possibility.

2b.   **MONARCHIST.** The secret is in the four products

$$NO \times N = RN \qquad (1)$$
$$NO \times H = ONH \qquad (2)$$
$$NO \times S = OHS \qquad (3)$$
$$NO \times A = HA \qquad (4)$$

Only 1 and 6 can be multiplied by more than two different digits and get those digits in the units. If O = 6, then from (2) N ≥ 7, giving three digits for the product in (1); thus O = 1.
Only 21×2 and 31×3 give two-digit products for NO × N, but the only products of 31 in the 100s are 124, 155 and 186 which do not fit the pattern of ONH. Hence N = 2 and R = 4.

   21 × H and 12H so H = 6.
   21 × S = 16S so S = 8.
   21 × A = 6A so A = 3.

We now have the quotient and the remainder; multiplying back, $21 \times 2683 + 6 = 56349$. Hence C = 5, T = 9.
Since $(A + 10) - H = I$, I = 7. The final M comes from the title!

2c. **Carol, the blonde, spent $8.70; Alison, the brunette, $4.35; and Maria, the redhead, $1.45.** If Maria spent x cents, then Alison spent $3x$ cents and Carol $6x$ cents. 725 cannot be $2x$ or $3x$ since neither 2 nor 3 are factors. Hence $5x = 725$ and $x = 145$.

2d. If $BC = x$ units and AC divides the area in half, then the area below AC is the triangle ABC plus a unit square; hence

$2(2x + 1) = 9$

$4x = 7$

so $BC = 1\frac{3}{4}$ units.

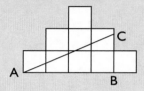

2e. $1 = (5 \div 5) \times (5 \div 5)$ $6 = (5 \times 5 + 5) \div 5$
$2 = (5 \div 5) + (5 \div 5)$ $7 = (5 + 5) \div 5 + 5$
$3 = (5 + 5 + 5) \div 5$ $8 = 5.5 + (5 \times .5)$
$4 = (5 \times 5 - 5) \div 5$ $9 = 5 + 5 - (5 \div 5)$
$5 = (5 - 5) \times 5 + 5$ $10 = 5 + 5 + 5 - 5$

2f. **Anne is in purchasing, Barbara in marketing and Donna in sales.** Since Anne did not earn the most and Barbara has a brother, the woman in sales is Donna. Anne is not in marketing.

2g. **A = 3, B = 7, C = 1, D = 0.** C is a 'carry' figure to the thousands, so C = 1. From the hundreds $A + B = 10$ as there is a carry from the tens, so D = 0. Thus $CCC \div A = AB$ and the only single-digit factor of 111 is 3, so A = 3 and B = 7. $1110 = 333 + 777 = 3 \times 370$.

2h. **There are 24 people at the tea table.** $\frac{3}{4}$ take milk and $\frac{1}{2}$ take sugar. Since $\frac{1}{3}$ take both, $\frac{3}{4} + \frac{1}{2} - \frac{1}{3} = \frac{11}{12}$ take either milk, sugar or both, leaving $\frac{1}{12}$ who take neither.

3a. If the square is 2 units by 2 units, then the area of the square equivalent to the whole shape is 5 square units, so the side has length $\sqrt{5}$ units. This length is that of the hypotenuse of a right-angled triangle with shorter sides of lengths 1 and 2 units. By rotating DAE 90° clockwise about D, and FEB 90° counter-clockwise about F, the required square is obtained.

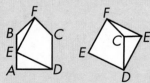

3b. **Pete, Pat, Pet; Pete, Pet, Pat; Pet, Pete, Pat; Pet, Pat, Pete; Pat, Pet, Pete; Pat, Pete, Pet.**

3c. **x = 20.** We want the nearest possible to equal divisions between the schools. $250 \div 13 = 19$ with a remainder of 3. Hence three schools would have 20 entries each, and the rest 19 each.

3d. **A = 4, E = 8, N = 9, O = 3, T = 2.** $A \times T \leq N$ (a single digit) and neither A nor T is 1 (since $A \times T = E$). $T \neq 3$ as that would make A = 2 and $2 \times O$ odd. If T = 4, then A = 2 and O must be 7 (using the tens) which gives a contradiction in the hundreds. Hence T = 2. If A = 3, O = 4 and again there is a contradiction in the hundreds, so A = 4 and the rest follows. $2332 \times 4 = 9328$.

3e. **There were two new stations.** If n and s are the numbers of old and new stations respectively, then the number of tickets rose from $n(n-1)$ to $(n+s)(n+s-1)$.

Hence
$$((n+s)^2 - (n+s)) - (n^2 - n) = 46$$
$$((n+s)^2 - n^2)) - ((n+s-n) = 46$$
$$s(2n+s) - s = 46$$
$$s(2n+s-1) = 46$$

but 46 can only be factorised as 2×23 or 1×46 (smaller factor first), and $s > 1$ since the number of new stations is stated in the plural.

Hence $s = 2$, so $n = 11$ and the number of tickets rose from 110 to 156.

3f. **There are three buses an hour into the city.** The bus leaving the city passes the third bus into the city after 30 minutes; only those three will arrive in the city in the first 60 minutes, since the third bus will take 30 minutes from the time it meets the outward bus.

3g. **Miss Ang is the manager, Miss Bundy the cashier, Mr Casey the floorwalker, Mr Dupont the buyer and Mr Evans the clerk.** Since the buyer is a bachelor he must be Mr Dupont or Mr Evans, but one of them must be the cashier or the clerk (an unmarried male is needed) and Mr Dupont is the best man, not the groom, so Mr Dupont is the buyer. As he is not the cashier, clerk or manager, Mr Cosey is the floorwalker. Mr Evans cannot be going to marry Miss Ang who is thus the manager, nor was he her roommate, so Mr Evans is the clerk and will marry Miss Bundy the cashier.

3h. **Mr Cheung has three red and 10 black cards, Mrs Cheung five red and eight black, Mr Singh seven red and six black, and Mrs Singh 11 red and two black cards.** If Mr Cheung has x red cards, Mrs Cheung y red cards and Mr Singh z red cards, they will have $13 - x$, $13 - y$ and $13 - z$ black cards respectively. Mrs Singh will have $26 - (x + y + z)$ red cards and $(x + y + z) - 13$ black cards. The Cheungs together hold $(x + y)$ red cards and the Singhs together hold $26 - (x + y)$ red cards. From the information given we have
$$26 - (x + y) = (x + y) + (13 - x)$$
i.e. $\quad 13 - 2y = x \quad$ (1)
and $\quad 13 - z = 2x \quad$ (2)
hence, from (1) and (2),
$$z = 4y - 13.$$
But y and z range from 0 to 13, so $y = 4$, 5 or 6. $y \neq 6$ since Mr Cheung holds at least 2 red cards, and $y \neq 4$ since Mrs Singh would then have 14 red cards! Hence $y = 5$, $z = 7$ and $x = 3$.

4a. **The footpath is 29 metres long.** The area without the footpath is $441 - 21 = 420 = 20 \times 21$ m^2. Hence each remaining triangle has its shorter sides 20 m and 21 m, so by Pythagoras's theorem the length of the footpath is $\sqrt{(20^2 + 21^2)} = 29$ m.

4b. **The keyword is HYSTERICAL.** From the additions at each end R + E = L, so H = 0 from the tens. Hence from the thousands, Y = 1 and from the hundred thousands R + R + 1 = 11 (there must be a 'carry' since Y is odd), so R = 5.

From the hundreds I + 5 = 11 and I = 6.

From the millions 6 + E + 1 = 11 and E = 4, so L = 5 + 4 = 9.

T + T + 1 = C (no carry), so C = 7 and T = 3.

From the ten thousands S + A = 10, but our keyword is already HY_TERIC_L, so A = 8 and S = 2.

$$\begin{array}{r} 536{,}520{,}604 \\ +\ 434{,}580{,}565 \\ \hline 971{,}101{,}169 \end{array}$$

4c. **The explorer takes twelve days.** On the first trip (two days) he goes one day, drops two water bottles and returns. On the second trip (four days) he goes two days, drops one water bottle and returns, picking up one water bottle from the first trip. He can now cross the desert (six days) by replacing his first two days' supply with those dropped earlier.

4d. **25 cows would last 40 days.** If the field initially contains A units of feed, where a cow eats 1 unit per day and the grass grows at q units per day, then

$$A + 20q = 40 \times 20, \text{ and}$$
$$A + 30q = 30 \times 30$$

Subtracting, $10q = 100$, so the grass would grow enough each day to feed 10 cows and the field had 600 units to start with. If the 25 cows take r days,

$$600 + 10r = 25r, \text{ which gives the result.}$$

A non-algebraic solution, (not altogether convincing, even though correct as far as it goes) is to note that $800 = 20 \times 40$ units last 20 days; $900 = 30 \times 30$ units lasts 30 days, so $1000 = 40 \times 25$ units will last 40 days. If we continue, $1100 = 50 \times 22$ units will last 50 days, that is 22 cows would last 50 days.

4e. **D = 9, E = 8, F = 2, I = 6, P = 0, T = 7, U = 5, V = 3, W = 1.**

We first write the two products

$$DI \times V = FEE \quad (1)$$
and $$DI \times E = TIE \quad (2)$$

None of I, V and E are 1 as each product has three digits and $I \times V = \_E$ in (1). This equation shows also that $E \neq 5$.

The only way that $I \times E = \_E$ in (2) is for I = 6 with E = 2, 4 or 8, but from the first subtraction E > I, so E = 8.

From the second subtraction E = T + 1, so T = 7 and from (2) D = 9.

From (1) V = 3 and F = 2; the rest follow immediately.

$96 \times 38 + 50 = 3698$.

4f. **The jars were 30 cm and 15 cm deep.** If the depth of the smaller jar is x cm, then

$$2x - 20 = 2(20 - x)$$
$$4x = 60$$

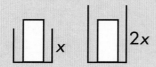

4g. **(i) Eleanor is a Neah. (ii) Rehto is a Yeah.** In the first problem Gordon is a Yeah and Eleanor is different, or a Neah and Eleanor is the same. In the second, Rehto did ask the question!

4h. **No. Since there are only four 1-unit equilateral triangles in one of side 2 units, two of the five points must be in the same unit triangle and so not more than 1 unit apart.**

5a. **I = 5, L = 9, S = 4, T = 0.**
From the ones, T = 0.
There is thus a 'carry' to the hundreds (I – I), so L = 9, and there is a carry to the thousands.
Hence from the thousands 9 – S – 1 = S, giving S = 4.
From the tens I = 5. 9540 – 4590 = 4950.

5b. **Boris is a sane human and Carlo a sane vampire.** Anyone who says 'I am human' is sane (whether human or vampire), so Boris' second statement is true. Boris is thus the human.

5c. **There are four distinct sequences, and another four which are their reverse:**
    ABC ACB CBA BAC BCA CAB
    ABC ACB CAB CBA BCA BAC
    ABC BAC ACB CBA BCA CAB
    ABC BCA BAC ACB CBA CAB
(The reverse sequence of the first one starts with CBA reversed: ABC BCA CBA BAC ACB CAB; the others are similarly obtained.)

5d. **Five subjects were represented.** If there are *n* subjects represented, each subject appears in (*n* – 1) pairs, so (*n* – 1) = 4, since there is a student for each pair. There are 10 students: if the subjects are a, b, c, d, e, then the pairs are ab, ac, ad, ae, bc, bd, be, cd, ce and de.

5e. **D = 7, E = 5, M = 1, N = 6, O = 0, R = 8, S = 9, Y = 2.**
M = 1 (only a 'carry'), so O = 0 and S = 8 or 9 from the thousands.
If there is a carry from the hundreds N = 0, so there is no carry,
S = 9 and N = E + 1.
Hence from the tens (E + 1) + R + carry from the ones = 10 + E,
so R + carry = 9 giving R = 8 and a carry of 1.
N < 8, so E < 7 and from the ones 12 ≤ D + E ≤ 13, so D = 7.
E ≠ 6 (which gives N = 7), so E = 5, N = 6 and Y = 2.
9567 + 1085 = 10,652.

5f. **Kaimana: v. Barham 7–3, v. Potridge 6–4, v. Sapford 0–10;**
     Barham: v. Potridge 5–5, v. Sapford 9–1; Potridge: v. Sapford 8–2.

There was only one draw since scores were different, and with six matches played the total in each match was (13 + 17 + 17 + 13) ÷ 6 = 10.

Potridge's results are therefore 5–5 v. Barham, 8–2 v. Sapford and 4–6 v. Kaimana. Barham therefore has a goal tally of 12–8 for its other two matches, so must have results 9–1 and 3–7.

Kaimana's remaining goal tally is 7–13 with results 7–3 and 0–10.

Hence Kaimana beat Barham 7–3 and the rest follows easily.

5g. **If a, b, g and s represent each adult, boy, girl and suitcase, the following six return trips will get all of them across and the ferry back:**

Left bank	River	Right bank
aas	bg →	
aas	← b	g
abs	a →	g
abs	← g	a
as	bg →	a
as	← b	ag
bs	a →	ag
bs	← g	aa
s	bg →	aa
s	← b	aag
	bs →	aag
	← b	aags

5h. Since there are 17 unit squares, the size of the required single square is √17 units, which is the length of the diagonal of a rectangle 4 units by 1 unit. The cuts form four identical pieces, which can be combined with the unit square as shown.

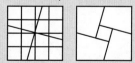

6a. **H = 7, N = 4, O = 2, R = 6, T = 5, E = 0**, since no other pattern gives EE in the product; hence the problem reduces to ON × ON = THR.

N ≠ 0 or 1 (N × N = _R) and O × O ≤ T. 32 × 32 has four digits, so O = 1 or 2.

Since H is odd, N × N has an odd number of tens; N ≠ R so N = 4.

But 14 × 14 = 196 and O ≠ T, so O = 2.

240 × 240 = 57,600.

6b. **It would have taken $4\frac{4}{9}$ hours (about 4 hours and 27 minutes).** If r is the part of a vat that a red tap fills in an hour, and b is the part that a black tap fills in an hour,

$$4r + 3b = \tfrac{1}{5}$$

and $\qquad 4r + 5b = \tfrac{1}{4}$

so $\qquad 2b = \tfrac{1}{4} - \tfrac{1}{5} = \tfrac{1}{20}$

hence $b = \tfrac{1}{40}$ and substituting:

$$4r = \tfrac{1}{5} - \tfrac{3}{40} = \tfrac{5}{40} = \tfrac{1}{8}$$

so $\qquad r = \tfrac{1}{32}$.

The amount filled in an hour by four red taps and four black taps is thus

$$\tfrac{4}{40} + \tfrac{4}{32} = \tfrac{1}{10} + \tfrac{1}{8} = \tfrac{9}{40}$$

so it takes $\tfrac{40}{9}$ hours to fill.

6c. **Peter gets 10 kiwifruit, 4 apples and 6 pears; Bonny gets 20 apples; and Don gets five kiwifruit, 12 apples and three pears.** No other combinations give 20 pieces of fruit for $5. (With 15 or more kiwifruit, there are too many pieces.)

6d. **Each number is two higher than it should be.** From the ones '2' = 0, from the hundreds '8' = '9' − 1 and there is a 'carry' from the tens. Hence from the tens, ('8' + 1) + '8' = 10 + '5' and from the thousands (no carry) 2 × '5' = '8'. Substituting,

$$4 \times \text{'5'} + 1 = 10 + \text{'5'}$$
$$3 \times \text{'5'} = 9.$$

So '5' = 3, '8' = 6 and '9' = 7. 3670 + 3067 = 6737.

6e. **Mr Smith is the teacher, Mrs Smith the lawyer, Mrs Smith's father the minister, Gwen the grocer and Alan the postmaster.** Alan is not the teacher or the lawyer since he is related by blood to all of the others. If Mrs Smith is the grocer, then Mr Smith must be the teacher as Mrs Smith's father is older than she is. That would make Mrs Smith's father both the minister (male) and the lawyer (not a blood relative). Hence Gwen is the grocer and Mr Smith the teacher. Mrs Smith's father is the minister, Mrs Smith the lawyer and Alan the postmaster.

6f. **The contact point is 42 cm above the ground.**

$BC = CT = 70$ cm, $ON = OT = 30$ cm. By similar triangles,

$$\tfrac{PO}{PC} = \tfrac{NO}{BC} = \tfrac{30}{70}$$

So $\qquad \tfrac{PO}{PO+OC} = \tfrac{3}{7}$

$\qquad 7PO = 3PO + 300$ cm $\qquad$ (since $OC = OT + TC$)

$\qquad PO = 75$ cm

Also by similar triangles,

$$\tfrac{ST}{BC} = \tfrac{PT}{PC} = \tfrac{75+30}{75+100} = \tfrac{105}{175} = \tfrac{3}{5}$$

$\qquad ST = \tfrac{3}{5} \times 70 = 42$ cm.

A more direct method is to note that the increase in height from O divides the difference in radii in the ratio 3:7, so the height is $30 + \tfrac{3}{10} \times 40 = 42$ cm.

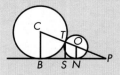

6g. **A club needs 10 yams, a lamp 8 yams and a fishhook 4 yams.** If c, l and f are the number of yams needed for each, then

$$2c = 3f + l \quad (1)$$

and $\quad 3c + 2l + f = 50 \quad (2)$

(1) can be written

$$4c - 2l - 6f = 0$$

and adding to (2)

$$7c - 5f = 50,$$

for which the smallest solution in whole numbers is $c = 10$, $f = 4$, the correct result. (The next pair up, $c = 15$, $f = 11$ makes l negative.)

6h. **The smallest value is $10\frac{1}{2}$.** Since A is in hundreds it will dominate so must be 1. The denominator needs to be as large as possible, so (as experiment will quickly verify) B and C are 8 and 9 respectively. The fraction is thus $\frac{189}{1+8+9}$.

7a. **One line is parallel to C (to make the right length) and the other is perpendicular to C intersecting the first line at the centre of the square at B to give it symmetry.**

7b. **There are 30 possible combinations.** Two of these have one symbol (a dot or a dash), $2^2 = 4$ have two, $2^3 = 8$ have three and $2^4 = 16$ have four symbols. The following four combinations are not used (there are only 26 letters in the alphabet):

$$- - - -, \; - - - \cdot, \; \cdot \cdot - - \;\; \text{and} \; \cdot - - \cdot \, .$$

7c. **Cardinals: draw v. Polygons, big wins v. Hyperbolas and Rationals; Polygons: win v. Hyperbolas, big win v. Rationals; Hyperbolas: win v. Rationals.** Cardinals must have had two big wins and a draw to get 29 points. Rationals had two big losses and a loss; Hyperbolas a win, a loss and a big loss. Polygons therefore must have drawn with Cardinals, leaving a big win (against Rationals, since Hyperbolas' big loss was to Cardinals) and a win against Hyperbolas. Hence Hyperbolas had a win against Rationals.

7d. **Mrs Tulip is 66 on her birthday.** Working backwards, she had 22 daffodils before they wilted, 33 before the grandchildren's game and 66 before she dropped half of them.

7e. **L = 7, O = 3, T = 6.** From the hundreds, since L is not T, L = T + 1 and the tens have 1 to 'carry' to the hundreds. From the ones, T = 2, 4, 6 or 8, but from the tens, T ≥ 5, so T = 6 or 8. If T = 8 then L = 9 so O = 4 in the ones, but 7 in the tens. Hence T = 6, L = 7 and O = 3. 73 + 663 = 736.

7f. **The message was at the intersection of corridors d and f.** The number of possible routes from an intersection is the sum of the numbers of routes from the two intersections immediately closer to the north-west corner. Building the numbers from the corner, there is only one intersection with 56 routes. (Note that the numbers make up Pascal's triangle.)

	A	B	C	D	E	F	G	H
	1	1	1	1	1	1	1	1
a								
b	1	2	3	4	5	6	7	8
c	1	3	6	10	15	21	28	36
d	1	4	10	20	35	56	84	120
e	1	5	15	35	70	126	210	330

7g. **A = 4, B = 1, M = 2, O = 6, R = 8, T = 3, Y = 7.**
From the two partial products:

$$MA \times T = YM \quad (1)$$
and $$MA \times O = BAA \quad (2)$$

From (2) M > B ≥ 1 and O ≠ 1.
From (1) T = 2, 3 or 4, M = 2, 3 or 4 and A ≠ 0 or 5.
From (2), since A × O = _A, O = 6 and A is even.
From (1) M is also even (2 or 4); if M = 4, T = 2 and A = 2 or 7 (odd). Hence M = 2, and from (1) A ≠ 8 since T would be 4 with a 3-digit product, so A = 4, T = 3 and Y = 7. From (2) B = 1, and from the first subtraction R – 2 = 6, so R = 8. 24 × 36 + 23 = 887.

7h. **A v. B: 1–2, A v. D: 0–0, A v. E: 3–0, C v. E: 3–4, D v. E: 3–2.** C can only have played one, and lost 3–4 to E. A must thus have played B, D and E. B played only one game, thus beat A 2–1. A's other games gave a goal tally of 3–0, so their draw was 0–0 and they beat E 3–0 (D did not have 3 goals scored against them, so they drew with A). D must therefore have played E with a score of 3–2 to D. The full table was:

	Played	Won	Lost	Drawn	Goals for	Goals against
A	3	1	1	1	4	2
B	1	1	0	0	2	1
C	1	0	1	0	3	4
D	2	1	0	1	3	2
E	3	1	2	0	6	9

8a. **The number is 42,857.** If the number is x, then

$10x + 1 = 3 (x + 100,000)$

$7x = 299,999$

$x = 42,857$.

Notice that with the 1 included, the numbers involved are 142,857 and 428,571, the numbers which recur in the decimals for $\frac{1}{7}$ and $\frac{3}{7}$. Hence the title!

8b. **A = 2, E = 0, L = 7, M = 4, R = 5, T = 8.** From the ones, A ≠ 1 and L ≠ 1, but from the thousands A × M ≤ T. If M = 1, A and L are 3 and 7 and there is a 'carry' of 2; but A × A ends in 9, so R = 1 = M. If M = 2, A = 3 or 4. If A = 3, L = 4 (from the ones), R = 0 (from the tens) and there is a carry of 1 to the hundreds so that 3 × E + 1 = _E, i.e. 2 × E = 9 or 19 which is impossible. If A = 4, L = 3 or 8, R = 7 or 9 and there is a carry of 1 to the hundreds. 4 × E + 1 = _E, i.e. 3 × E = 9, 19 or 29 whence E = 3, so L = 8 and R = 9; but from the thousands T = 4 × 2 + 1 = 9 also. Therefore M ≥ 3 and hence A = 2. Thus M = 4 (it must be even and less than 5), L = 7, R = 5, E = 0 and T = 8. 4027 × 2 = 8054.

8c. **The order of play was Anna, Bella, Cara, Dana (as stated) and the order of the dominoes was 6–5, 5–5, 5–4, 4–4, 6–6, 6–4, 6–3, 5–3.** Anna's dominoes are 6–6 and 6–5, Bella's 6–4 and 5–5, Cara's 6–3 and 5–4, and Dana's 5–3 and 4–4; these are the only possibilities with the totals given. The order is obtained by trial: for instance, if the first four dominoes are 6–6, 6–4, 6–3 and 4–4, Anna cannot play her second domino. Some of the chains are quite long, but it is soon established that Anna must start 6–5. The full chain (with A1 denoting Anna's first domino etc.) is:

D2	C2	A2	A1	B1	C1	D1	B2
5–3	3–6	6–6	6–5	5–5	5–4	4–4	4–6.

or	A2	A1	B1	C1	D1	B2	C2	D2
	6–6	6–5	5–5	5–4	4–4	4–6	6–3	3–5.

8d. **The table has a diameter of 1.46 m (146 cm).** If the radius is r cm, then the sides of the rectangle have length $(r - 18)$ and $(r - 25)$ cm.

Hence, using Pythagoras's theorem,

$(r - 18)^2 + (r - 25)^2 = r^2$

$r^2 - 86r + 949 = 0$

$(r - 73)(r - 13) = 0$.

$r \neq 13$ as the rectangle would then have negative dimensions; so $r = 73$.

8e. **E should receive the parcel.** The solution is quite straightforward by trial. If A receives the parcel, the ninth person is B (second time round) the next to go (remember B is eliminated) is E, then C, D, A and F, leaving G to go free. Thus if the receiver is three to the right of A (E), the person to go free will be three to the right of G (i.e. D).

8f. The word is **HYDROMATIC**.

$Y = 1$ ($Y \times$ DOOR = DOOR) and H = 0.

Since TRDC = DOOR $\times$ R has only 4 digits, R $\times$ D $\leq$ T. If R = 2, C = 4 so D = 3, but D = 2 $\times$ O which is even. If R = 4, D = 2 and C = 6 and there is a 'carry' of 1 making D odd. Hence R = 3, D = 2, and C = 9. 3 $\times$ O = _2, so O = 4 and T = 7. The keyword can now be guessed: HYDRO_ _T_C. Alternatively, add the tens: 1 + 4 = _2, so I = 8 and using the tens multiplier, A $\times$ 3 = _8 giving A = 6 and 6 $\times$ 4 + 1 = _M, so M = 5. 2443 $\times$ 361 = 881,923.

8g. **There were 135 starlings on the tree originally.** The answer can be obtained by working backwards:

8 ➞ 16 ➞ 9; 9 ➞ 18 ➞ 11 etc., but a quicker way is to note the seven halvings, so the answer is related to 2^7.

By adding 7 to match the birds arriving, the pattern is maintained:

$(2^7 + 7 + 7) \div 2 = 2^6 + 7$

$(2^6 + 7 + 7) \div 2 = 2^5 + 7$

and so on until

$(2^1 + 7 + 7) \div 2 = 8$

hence there were 128 + 7 = 135 birds. Note that the sequence goes no further. Why?

8h. **Polly's block was 80 m by 60 m, and Peter's was 96 m by 28 m.** If the sides of a block are x metres and y metres long, then by Pythagoras's theorem

$$x^2 + y^2 = 100^2$$

This is only possible if both x and y are multiples of 4, since 100^2 is a multiple of 16, which cannot happen with either odd numbers or odd multiples of 2 (try it). Let $x = 4u$ and $y = 4v$; then

$$u^2 + v^2 = 25^2$$

and the larger of u and v is more than $\sqrt{\frac{625}{2}}$, or at least 18, since it is a whole number. The quickest path to the answers is to take u = 18, 19 … 24, getting only u = 20, v = 15 and u = 24, v = 7 as whole number solutions. Hence the blocks have dimensions ($4u$ by $4v$) 80 m by 60 m (= 4800 m^2) and 96 m by 28 m (= 2688 m^2).

9a. **The keyword is REGULATION.** E = 1, since ALTER $\times$ E = ALTER, and R = 0 as R + E = E in the tens. Multiplying by T gives T $\times$ T = _T, so T = 5 or 6, but adding the hundreds, T + T = _G and G $\neq$ 0, so T = 6 and G = 2.

Thus, continuing to multiply by T gives 6 $\times$ L + 3 = _I, so L = 4, 5, 7 or 9, but (from the hundred millions) A = L + 1, so L $\neq$ 5 or 9, leaving L = 4 or 7. Multiplying by 0 gives O $\times$ 6 = _O, with O = 4 or 8 with a 'carry' of 2 or 4, and O $\times$ L + carry = _6; this is not possible for L = 7 (it makes O = 2 or 6), so L = 4, A = 5, I = 7 and O must be 8.

The keyword so far is REG_LATIO_, so U = 3, and N = 9.

54,610 $\times$ 9861 = 538,509,210.

9b. **Mary collects coins, Alan collects stamps and Rana collects butterflies.** Neither Mary nor Rana is the spy, so the spy must be Alan. Alan thus is not the lepidopterist or the numismatist, so collects stamps. Mary must therefore be the numismatist and hence Rana the lepidopterist. Note that there is not enough information to determine the other professions.

9c. **2 cylinders and 3 cones balance 10 cubes.** If a cylinder weighs the same as y cubes and a cone the same as o cubes, then

$$2y = 3o + 1$$

and $\quad 5o = 2y + 2.$

Hence

$$5o - 2 = 3o + 1$$

giving $o = 1\tfrac{1}{2}$

hence $2y = 5\tfrac{1}{2}$, leaving $3o = 4\tfrac{1}{2}$ and $2y + 3o = 10$.

9d. **The diagram shows a solution with five points.** If there are six points, there are five lines from any point, so at least three lines of the same colour – say AB, AC and AD – are all red. But then BC, BD and CD must all be blue and triangle BCD would be blue. Hence six points cannot be joined as required.

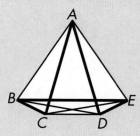

9e. **Eric handed over $5.50.** Since there are only multiples of 10 cents, there will be an even number of 45-cent stamps, so consider them as two for 90 cents. We need to find the maximum number a (lots of 10-cent pieces) such that if p and q pairs are the number of stamps,

$$8p + 9q = a$$

cannot be solved in whole numbers. This number is 55 as from then on we get a pattern without gaps as follows:

$8 \times 7 + 9 \times 0 = 56$
$8 \times 6 + 9 \times 1 = 57$
$8 \times 5 + 9 \times 2 = 58$
$8 \times 4 + 9 \times 3 = 59$
$8 \times 3 + 9 \times 4 = 60$
$8 \times 2 + 9 \times 5 = 61$
$8 \times 1 + 9 \times 6 = 62$
$8 \times 0 + 9 \times 7 = 63$
$8 \times 8 + 9 \times 0 = 64$
$8 \times 7 + 9 \times 1 = 65$

...

$5.60 is thus made up of $7 \times$ 80-cent stamps, $5.70 of one pair of 45-cent and $6 \times$ 80-cent stamps and so on. (If stamps of both denominations are required, the maximum 'impossible' amount is $7.20.)

9f. **Mr Robbie is Peter, Mrs Robbie is Sally and the children are Harry and Gwen.** Call the statements a, b, c, d. If b is true, a must also be true, as must one of c and d; hence b is false.

If c is true, Harry and Sally are the children making all the other statements false, *or* father and daughter so a and b are also true, *or* husband and wife with b and d also true.

Hence c is also false and the true statements are a and d.

9g. **(a) Pairings can be made in 9 ways. (b) There are 27 possible matches.**
If upper-case letters represent husbands and lower-case letters represent wives, partners can be

Ab, Ba, Cd, Dc

Ab, Bc, Cd, Da

Ab, Bd, Ca, Dc

and similar sets with Ac and Ad, making 9 in all. Each set of four pairs can be matched in 3 different ways, so 27 matches are possible.

9h. **M = 9, C = 4, I = 7.** $M \neq 0$, so from the tens M = 9 and there is a 'carry' from the ones. From the hundreds, C = 4 and from the ones I = 7.
447 + 497 = 944.

10a.

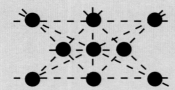

10b. Since the numbers add up to 78, which is not divisible by 4, the IX must be separated to I and X, changing 9 to 11 and the total to $80 = 4 \times 20$. (Other divisions are possible using the same principle.)

10c. **4 boxes and 24 loose eggs.** If x is the weekly number of boxes, y the weekly number of loose eggs, and z the number of boxes into which the loose eggs were placed,

$y = 6x$ and

$x = 6y - 20z$.

Hence $x = 36x - 20z$

$20z = 35x$

$4z = 7x$.

The smallest solution is $x = 4$, $z = 7$, with $y = 24$. Multiples of this set make the number of loose eggs too large.

10d. **The husbands and tennis partners in order were:**

Wife	Husband	Tennis partner
Alice	George	Frank
Betty	Henry	Ed
Carol	Frank	Henry
Dorothy	Ed	George

Ed was not married to Betty, Carol or Alice, so was Dorothy's husband. Hence George partnered Dorothy, so was Alice's husband. Therefore Carol's husband was Frank who partnered Alice. Henry thus partnered Carol and his wife was Betty.

10e.

Since the cross has five unit squares, the side of the square of area equal to that of the cross is 5, which is the hypotenuse of a right-angled triangle with shorter sides 1 and 2. Since the pieces are identical, the required cuts pass through the centre of the cross.

10f. **A = 5, B = 2, E = 4, H = 6, N = 1, O = 3, T = 7.** N = 1 since BET × N = BET. O × T = _1, so O and T are 3 and 7 with a 'carry' of 2 to the hundreds. O ≠ 7, since O × BET has only three digits.
Hence O = 3, T = 7 and 3 × B ≤ 7, so B = 2, with a carry of 1 from the hundreds. From the hundreds 3 × E + 2 = 10 + E, so E = 4; adding, A = 5 and H = 6.
247 × 31 = 7657.

10g. **80 m by 130 m and 130 m by 160 m.** Since the fields have a common side, the other side of the larger field is twice the length of that of the smaller (having double the area). It is also 30 m + 50 m = 80 m longer. Hence the smaller field has its shorter side 80 m long and the common side either 110 m or 130 m long. (The other pair of fields are 80 m by 110 m and 110 m by 160 m.)

10h. **If she had seen two black dots, hers was white; if a black dot and a white dot and hers was black, the one with a white dot would have known; both of these deductions would have been rapid. Hence she saw two white dots, and realised that the others must also be seeing two white dots, so hers was also white.**

Bogglers

Bogglers are longer and often harder even though they require no more mathematical knowledge. Again there is a hint for each question, and full answers with explanations are provided.

Bogglers

Bogglers are longer and often harder even though they require no more mathematical knowledge. Again there is a hint for each question, and full answers with explanations are provided.

1.   Around the table

From the following statements, find the names, occupations and seating arrangements of the six friends:

1.   Mr and Mrs Smith, Mr and Mrs Brown and Mr and Mrs Green were seated (equally spaced) around a circular table.

2.   No man is sitting next to his wife, but each woman has a man on either side of her.

3.   The names in no particular order are Joan, Mary, Nancy, Dick, Harry and Tom.

4.   The occupations of the men are architect, singer and politician, and those of the women are teacher, engineer and artist.

5.   Dick and Mr Smith often play bridge with the architect's wife and Mrs Green.

6.   The singer, who is an only child, has Mary on his right.

7.   The politician is sitting nearer to Nancy than he is to Mrs Brown.

8.   Harry is the architect's brother-in-law and is sitting on the right of his only sister.

9.   The architect has no sisters.

10.   The artist is opposite the architect and Dick is next to the engineer.

2. The primary cube

In how many ways can
you colour the faces
of a cube with
each side
coloured red,
green or blue?

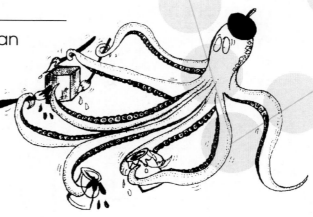

3. Daddy, daddy!

Four fathers and their four daughters have to cross a river.
There is a boat which holds three people. Although all can
row, no daughter is prepared to be with another man
unless her father is also present.
How can they all cross the river?

4. Pregnant hind caught

In this alphametic the digits 0 to 9 in order are represented by a keyword. Find it.

```
    R O P E
    D E E R
+   T R A P
  ─────────
    A N I P A
+ I N S I D E
  ─────────
  I S R T D D
```

5. The digger's claim

In the gold-rush days a gold-digger carried a rope which was 2 chains (about 40 metres) long and some pegs. If he was allowed to mark out a square claim of up to 3 square chains, show how he could use his equipment to get the maximum area allowed. (The rope may be used as a straight-edge or as a compass.)

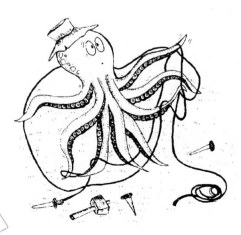

6.   Top scholars

In awarding a scholarship for which there were five candidates, credit was allocated as follows: 5 points for the top mark in each of five subjects, 4 points for the second mark and so on.

All five candidates came top in one subject.

Angela won the scholarship with 18 points; Brian was 2 points behind followed by Colin, Debbie and Edgar in that order.

Angela was first in mathematics.

Brian came first in physics and third both in French and English.

Colin was first in English, second in biology and third in mathematics.

Edgar was first in biology and second in French.

Find where each candidate came in every subject.

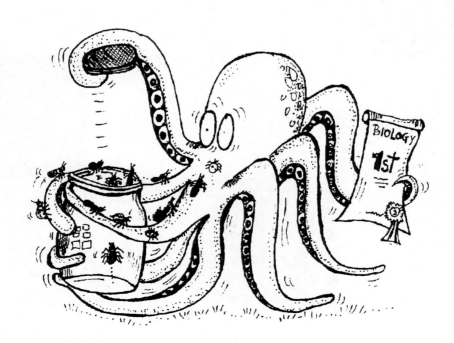

7. A product crossword

If every letter of the solution is given its position in the alphabet as a number (with A = 1, B = 2, C = 3 and so on), then the clues are the products for each word.

(For example, the clue for M A D would be 13 × 1 × 4 = 52; the clue for D A M would also be 52.)

Clues across
1. 285
4. 360
6. 810
7. 60

Clues down
2. 270
3. 20
5. 360
6. 54

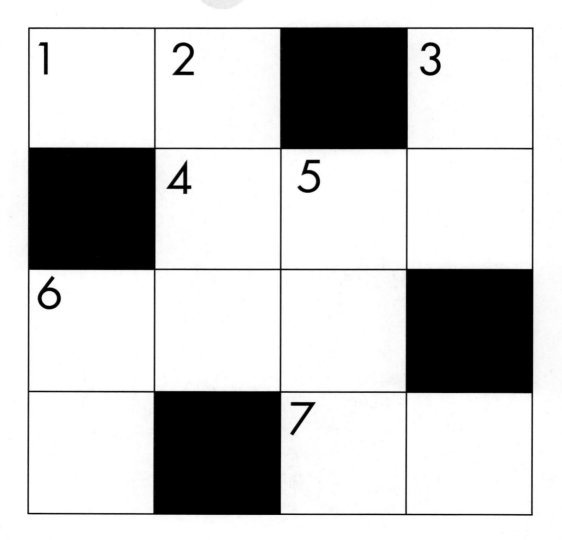

8.   Disharmony of the spheres

One of the twelve otherwise identical balls has a weight different from that of the others.
You have just three weighings on a balance to discover which one is different and whether it is heavier or lighter than the others.

9.   Roman roads

Straight roads join Aid, Bead, Cede and Deed, with the distances between the townships being a whole number of kilometres.
If Cede is the same distance from Aid and Bead, and Deed is 11 km from Bead on the road to Aid and equidistant from Aid and Cede, what is the distance from Aid to Bead?

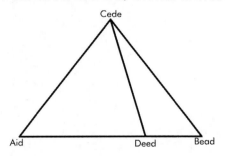

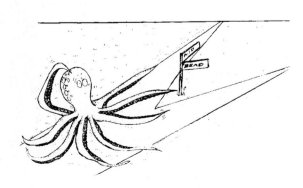

---

10. They're off!

There are six horses in the race.

Asher and Elf's Fury are paying $10 for a win, Beecham $9, and Flagging and Catch Up each $8, while the favourite, Dodgem, is paying $2.40.

Place the bets for Mr Winalot so that he has a net win of $40 whichever horse wins the race.

Mr Winalot is already a millionaire, so there is no limit on the bets.

(To state that a horse pays $5 means that the successful punter receives $5 for each dollar staked; the stake is not returned.)

11. They all need a garage

Six couples live in a short street with nos 1, 3 and 5 opposite nos 2, 4 and 6 respectively.

Goldie lives next door to the Audi car and John next to the Holden.

Sapphira lives between Edward and the Ford and opposite Ruby.

Beryl, who has the Toyota, lives opposite William, while Henry with his Lada lives opposite Pearl.

Robert at no. 1 does not have a Ford, but lives opposite Amber who can see her next-door neighbour's Jaguar.

Which car belongs to Richard, and who is his partner?

12. Don't forget the key

Mr Jones the farmer walks from his house (*H*) to his barn (*B*) by the path which runs clockwise round the edge of his 100-metre-square paddock.

At the same time his daughter Tammy runs from the house to the first corner (*A*), then returns to get the key to the barn (which she had forgotten).

Tammy gives her father the key when she catches up with him along the second side (at *X*) and returns to the house at the same time that Mr Jones arrives at the barn.

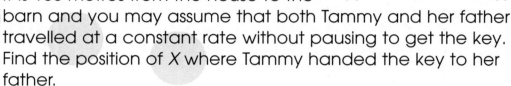

It is 165 metres from the house to the barn and you may assume that both Tammy and her father travelled at a constant rate without pausing to get the key. Find the position of *X* where Tammy handed the key to her father.

13. Four into one makes five

Four straight cuts divide a square into nine pieces.
If these pieces can be rearranged to make five identical small squares, where are the cuts?

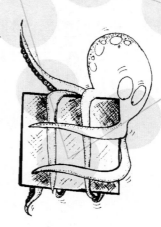

14. Points for polo

In a water polo competition 10 points are awarded for a win, 5 points for a draw and a bonus of 1 point for each goal scored regardless of the result.
Ayford finished up, after each team had played the others once, with 34 points, Beeford 25, Seaford 20 and Deeford only 6. If every result was different and all sides scored in each match, find those scores.

15. A cross-number puzzle

Clues across
1. An odd multiple of 13
3. One less than a square
4. A cube
6. 1 down minus 8-across
8. The product of two primes
9. A number between 1-across and 5-down

Clues down
1. A square
2. A multiple of the sum of the digits in 1-across
3. A multiple of 9
5. The square of 8-across
7. A multiple of 6-across
8. The square of the difference between the digits of 1-down

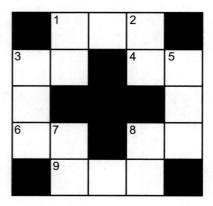

16. Big squares, little squares

A 10-by-10 square grid produces 100 unit squares, but many more if larger squares are counted (385 all told).

What is the smallest number of unit squares which form a rectangular grid whose total number of squares is exactly 100?

(For example, the grid shown below has 12 + 6 + 2 = 20 squares.)

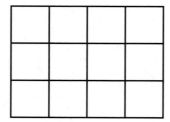

17.   Who wrote Gray's *Elegy*?

At a very old churchyard in England I found the following headstone in a graveyard:

Robert ----------

b. Oct 1 ++++++++++

d. Nov 27 +++++++++

Aged 51 years

And his wife Alice who died three months later

b. Feb 2 +++++++++

d. Feb 27 +++++++

Aged 36 years

The illegible dates used Roman numerals, with each + representing one of the letters I, V, X, L, C, D, M.
What were the actual dates?

18. Just answer the questions

On the island of Koo (where the Goodies always tell the truth, the Fixers always lie and the Shilly-shallies alternately lie and tell the truth) I asked Rag, Tag and Bobtail two questions each, to which their replies were as follows:

Rag: Tag and I are the same; Tag and Bobtail are the same.

Tag: Bobtail and I are different; Rag and Bobtail are the same.

Bobtail: Rag and I are different; Rag and Tag are different.
Who belongs to which tribe?

19. The magic star of David

Place the numbers 1 to 12 so that each row of four numbers and the six points of the star all have the same total.

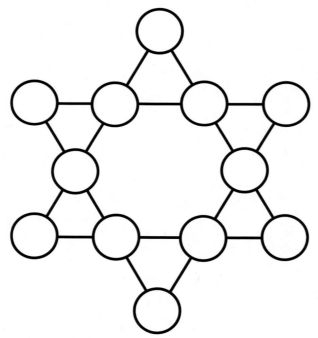

20. They could be dangerous

Nine prisoners are taken to the court each day handcuffed in groups of three (as shown below).
If the trial lasts six days and no prisoner is directly handcuffed to the same person more than once, how could that constraint be achieved?

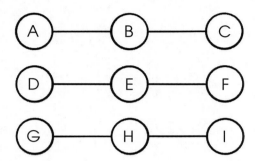

Hints for Bogglers

1. Each man is opposite his wife.

2. Work out with most (or equal most) of the sides being red, say, then check permutations of colours for each partition of the 6 sides – e.g. 4R, 1G, 1B.

3. All three in the boat can be fathers or daughters.

4. A = 1 or 2; show, using the ones and tens, that A + E < 10.

5. A 30°, 60°, 90° triangle has sides in the ratio 1:√3:2.

6. Each student has a different share of the total 75 points.

7. Go for 1 across and 2 down.

8. Specify whether each ball could be heavy or light. You need the maximum possible information from each weighing, whatever the result.

9. Use the bisector of angle *ACB* and Pythagoras's theorem.

10. The winning amount is always $40 more than the total staked.

11. Show that Sapphira and Ruby live in the middle houses.

12. The distances travelled in a given time by Tammy and Mr Jones are always in the same ratio.

13. Find a right-angled triangle with sides in the ratio 1:2:√5.

14. You can find out how many of the 60 points each team gets for *results*.

15. Use 8 down to help get 1 down and 3 across.

16. The shorter side of the rectangle is at most 6 units. Why?

17. The number of Roman numerals for the digits 0 to 9 are 0, 1, 2, 3, 2, 1, 2, 3, 4, 2.

18. Rag is not a Goodie; neither Tag nor Bobtail is a Fixer. Why?

19. Each number is counted twice in the rows, so you can find the magic total.

20. Each prisoner must spend two days in the middle.

Bogglers answers

1. **Harry and Joan Brown are the politician and the engineer; Dick and Nancy Green are the singer and the teacher; Tom and Mary Smith are the architect and the artist.** Statements 1 and 2 show that the order around the table is woman, man, woman, man, woman, man, and that each woman is opposite her husband.

   From 7 Mr Brown is the politician; from 5 Mr Green is not the architect so he is the singer and thus Mr Smith is the architect.

   From 5 and 8 Mr Smith is not Dick or Harry so is Tom; from 8 and 9 Harry is the architect's wife's brother, so Harry's only sister is Mrs Smith; thus from 6 Harry is not the singer who must therefore be Dick, with Harry the politician.

   From 8 the clockwise order of the men around the table must be Green, Smith, Brown, so from 6 and 10 Mary is Mrs Smith the artist; from 7 Nancy is Mrs Green and so from 3 and 10 Joan is Mrs Brown the engineer, with Nancy the teacher.

2. **There are 57 ways.** We consider only patterns having the most red sides then multiply the number of permutations of colours. For example 5R, 1G pattern has six, since there is also 5R, 1B; 5G, 1R; 5G, 1B; 5B, 1R; 5B, 1G.

Pattern	Perms.		No. ways on cube	
6R	3	×	1	
5R, 1G	6	×	1	
4R, 2G	6	×	2	G's opposite; G's adjacent
4R, 1G, 1B	3	×	2	GB opposite; GB adjacent
3R, 3G	3	×	2	Two R's opposite; all R's adjacent
3R, 2G, 1B	6	×	3	Two R's opposite, G's opposite; two R's opposite, G's adjacent; all R's adjacent
2R, 2G, 2B	1	×	6	all opposite; R's opposite, G, B adjacent; R's adjacent, G's opposite; R's adjacent, B's opposite; all adjacent – two ways

An alternative method is to make a grid of all possible numbers of red and green sides (the number of blue sides is then determined). The number inside each cell shows the number of ways in which the cube can be painted.

Red

Green \ Red	0	1	2	3	4	5	6
0	1	1	2	2	2	1	1
1	1	2	3	3	2	1	
2	2	3	6	3	2		
3	2	3	3	2			
4	2	2	2				
5	1	1					
6	1						

3. **They can all get across in nine trips – five outward and four returns.**
Call the fathers A, B, C, D and the daughters a, b, c, d respectively.

Near bank	River	Far bank
ABCDa	bcd →	
ABCDa	← bc	d
ABab	CDc →	d
ABab	← Cc	Dd
abc	ABC →	Dd
abc	← d	ABCD
a	bcd →	ABCD
a	← A	BCD bcd
	Aa →	BCD bcd

(The problem can be solved if the boat only holds two people, but only if there is an island in the river – see *The Moscow Puzzles* by Boris Kordemsky.)

4. **The keyword is PATRONISED.** A must be 1 or 2, since it is a carry from the thousands. If A + E ≥ 10, then D = 1 (since it cannot be 0), making A = 2 and E = 9; but then from the tens, P must also be 9. Hence A + E = D and P = 0. That means that E + R = 10 + A (units) and thus E + A + 1 = 10 (tens); so E + A = D = 9 and either A = 2, E = 7, R = 5 or A = 1, E = 8, R = 3. Assume A = 2. From the hundreds O + 7 + 5 + 1 = _I. If the 'carry' is 2, then O = 8 and I = 1, making T = 2 = A. Hence the carry is 1 and I = O + 3; I is not 6 (which gives T = 2) so I = 4, O = 1 and T = 8. This is a contradiction with the thousands which gives _N = R + D + T + 1 = 23, N = 3 and S = 2 = A. From the prolonged chain of argument, A = 1, E = 8, R = 3. Since O ≠ 8 or 9, O + 8 + 3 + 1 = 10 + I, or I = O + 2. O is not 2 (which gives T = 8 = E), nor is it 5 (which makes I = 7, T = 4 and _N = R + D + T + 1 = 17, i.e. N= 7 = I); hence O = 4, I = 6, T = 2. From the thousands, N = 5 and 5 + S + 1 = 13, so S = 7.
(Some short cuts can be made if the keyword is checked. For instance T ≠ 8 as no word ends in TD.)
ROPE = 3408, DEER = 9883, TRAP = 2310, ANIPA = 15,601, INSIDE = 657,698 and ISRTDD = 673,299.

5. **Straighten out the rope and mark the ends (*A*, *B* in the diagram). Fold the rope in two to get the midpoint *O* and drive a peg through the strands there. Scribe arcs with centre *O*, radius *OB* and centre *B*, radius *OB*, and mark the intersection at *C*; then angle *ACB* is a right angle and by Pythagoras's Theorem *AC* is the side of the required square. To complete the construction, scribe arcs with centre *O*, radius *OA* and centre *A* radius *OA* to get *D*; then measure the length *AC* along *CB* and *AD* to get *E* and *F* respectively. *ABEF* is the required square.**

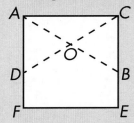

6.

Points:	5	4	3	2	1	Total
Angela	Maths	Physics English	Biology	French		18
Brian	Physics	Maths	French English		Biology	16
Colin	English	Biology	Maths	Physics	French	15
Debbie	French		Physics	Maths English Biology		14
Edgar	Biology	French			English Maths Physics	12

The only way to get 15 × 5 = 75 points altogether with all scores different was for Colin to have 15, Debbie 14 and Edgar 12.

Since everyone came first in a subject, Debbie was first in French. Edgar already had 9 points, so he must be last in his other three subjects.

Colin had only 3 points left, so was last in French and fourth in physics.

Hence Angela must be fourth in French, which leaves 11 points for her remaining subjects; so she was third in biology and second in Physics and English.

Brian could not thus have another third place, so was second in maths and last in biology.

Hence Debbie came third in physics and fourth in maths, English and biology.

7.

A B C D E F G H I J K L M N O P Q R S T U V W X Y Z
1 2 3 4 5 6 7 8 9 10 11 12 13 14 15 16 17 18 19 20 21 22 23 24 25 26

From 1-across 285 = 19 × 15, but 19 is not a factor of 2-down, so 1-across is SO and 2-down is O _ _ (remaining product 18) so is OAR (from the only letters which form a word).

6-across is now _R_ (remaining product 45) and must be IRE (ERI, ORC and CRO are not words), with 6-down IF.

4-across is A _ _ (remaining product 360 = 18 × 20), so is ART. The rest follows by division.

8. **First weighing: 1 2 3 4 against 5 6 7 8**, where each ball is given a number.
    Case (i): 1 2 3 4 > 5 6 7 8 (i.e. the pan containing 1 2 3 4 goes down). Denoting a heavy or a light ball by H or L, we have: 1H, 2H, 3H, 4H, 5L, 6L, 7L or 8L.
    Second weighing: 1 2 5 against 3 4 6.
    (a) 1 2 5 > 3 4 6 gives 1H, 2H or 6L.
    Third weighing: 1 against 2. 1 > 2: **1H**, 1 = 2: **6L**, 1 < 2: **2H**.
    (b) 1 2 5 = 3 4 6 gives 7L or 8L
    Third weighing: 7 against 8. 7 > 8: **8L**, 7 < 8: **7L**.
    (c) 1 2 5 < 3 4 6 gives 3H, 4H or 5L
    Third weighing 3 against 4. 3 > 4: **3H**, 3 = 4: **5L**, 3 < 4: **4H**.
    Case (ii): 1 2 3 4 = 5 6 7 8. The odd ball is 9, 10, 11 or 12.
    Second weighing: 6 7 8 against 9 10 11
    (a) 6 7 8 > 9 10 11 gives 9L, 10L or 11L
    Third weighing: 9 against 10. 9 > 10: **10L**, 9 = 10: **11L**, 9 < 10: **9L**.
    (b) 6 7 8 = 9 10 11 gives 12H or 12L
    Third weighing: 8 against 12. 8 > 12: **12L**, 8 < 12: **12H**.
    (c) 6 7 8 < 9 10 11 gives 9H, 10H or 11H
    Third weighing: 10 against 11. 10 > 11: **10H**, 10 = 11: **9H**, 10 < 11: **11H**.
    Case (iii): 1 2 3 4 < 5 6 7 8. This case is the precise reverse of case (i) and the second and third weighings are identical.

    1 > 2: **2L**, 1 = 2: **5H**, 1 < 2: **1L**;
    7 > 8: **7H**, 7 < 8: **8H**;
    3 > 4: **4L**, 3 = 4: **6H**, 3 < 4: **3L**.

    Apart from renumbering, there are other solutions. An interesting approach to the problem is given in Calvin Long's article 'Magic in Base 3' (*Mathematical Gazette* No. 477, November 1992). Can you show that it is impossible to repeat the argument if there are more than 12 balls?

9. **It is 36 km from Aid to Bead.**
    The townships are shown as *A, B, C, D* on the diagram;

    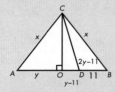

    If $AC = CB = x$ and $AO = y$, where O is the midpoint of AB, then $OD = y - 11$, and $CD = AD = 2y - 11$. We can now use Pythagoras's theorem to get two expressions for OC^2 in triangles AOC and DOC:
    $$OC^2 = x^2 - y^2 = (2y - 11)^2 - (y - 11)^2$$
    $$x^2 - y^2 = 3y^2 - 22y$$
    $$x^2 = 2y(2y - 11)$$
    Since 11 is prime, both $2y$ and $(2y - 11)$ must be perfect squares. The only such squares are 36 and 25, so $x = 30$, $y = 18$. A neat solution which requires no new line segments is as follows: Triangles ADC, ACB are similar since they have one of their base angles (angle BAC) in common. Hence
    $$\frac{x}{2y} = \frac{x}{2y}$$
    $$x^2 = 2y (2y - 11)$$
    etc.

10. **Stake as follows: Asher \$180, Beecham \$200, Catch Up \$225, Dodgem \$750, Elf's Fury \$180, Flagging \$225.** If \$$a$ is staked on Asher and Elf's Fury, \$$b$ on Beecham, \$$c$ on Catch Up and Flagging, and \$$d$ on Dodgem, then the total stake is

$$\$(2a + b + 2c + d)$$

so whichever horse wins must pay

$$\$(2a + b + 2c + d + 40) = \$x.$$

The winning payout of each horse is given, so

$$x = 10a = 9b = 8c = 2.4d$$

and $\quad x = \frac{2x}{10} + \frac{x}{9} + \frac{2x}{8} + \frac{10x}{24} + 40$

Thus $\quad 360x = 72x + 40x + 90x + 150x + 14{,}400$

$$8x = 14{,}400$$

giving $a = 180$, $b = 200$, $c = 225$ and $d = 750$.

To check, say the winner is Beecham: the stakes of \$1760 are forfeited, so there is a net win of $\$(200 \times 9) - \$1760 = \$40$.

(It is not generally known that it is possible to guarantee a win if the sum of the reciprocals of the win amounts is less than 1.)

Here we have

$$\frac{1}{10} + \frac{1}{10} + \frac{1}{9} + \frac{1}{8} + \frac{1}{2.4} = \frac{352}{360}$$

If we divide \$40 by what is left ($= \frac{8}{360}$) we get the money that the winning horse must pay. $\$40 \div \frac{8}{360} = \$40 \times 45 = \$1800$.)

11. **Richard has the Audi, his partner is Ruby.** Each statement has two parts; call them 1a, 1b, 2a, 2b, 3a, 3b, 4a, 4b.

From 2a and 4a, Sapphira lives at no. 4, since she is in a middle house and neither Edward nor the Ford is at no. 1.

From 2b Ruby must be at no. 3 and from 4b Amber is at no. 2 with Sapphira's Jaguar next door.

Goldie must live at an end house (the middle ones are occupied!), so from 1a the Audi is at no. 3 and Goldie is at no. 1 or no. 5.

From 3b Henry and his Lada are at no. 5, since nos 1, 2 and 6 are occupied by others (2a and 4a); Pearl is at no. 6.

From 3a Beryl and her Toyota are at no. 1 with William at no. 2 and Goldie at no. 5. From 2a Edward is at no. 6 and the Ford at no. 2.

The only car unplaced is the Holden, which must be at no. 6, so from 1b John is at no. 4, leaving Richard at no. 3.

1. Robert, Beryl, Toyota
2. William, Amber, Ford
3. Richard, Ruby, Audi
4. John, Sapphira, Jaguar
5. Henry, Goldie, Lada
6. Edward, Pearl, Holden

12. **X is 20 metres along the second side.** If $AX = x$ metres, then Tammy has travelled $(300 + x)$ metres while Mr Jones has travelled $(100 + x)$ metres. When Mr Jones reaches the barn he has travelled 165 metres and Tammy has travelled

$(300 + x) + (100 + x)$ metres

$= 400 + 2x$ metres

Their relative speeds are constant, so

$\frac{400 + 2x}{165} = \frac{300 + x}{100 + x}$

$40{,}000 + 400x + 200x + 2x^2 = 49{,}500 + 165x$

$2x^2 + 435x - 9500 = 0$

$(x - 20)(2x + 475) = 0$

so $x = 20$, being positive.

To check, Tammy travels 320 metres while Mr Jones travels 120 metres, and 440 metres while he travels 165 metres ($\frac{320}{120} = \frac{440}{165} = \frac{8}{3}$).

13.

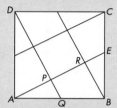

If the side of the square has length 2 units, then the area is 4 square units, so the area of each small square must be $\frac{4}{5}$ square units with the side

$\frac{2}{\sqrt{5}} = \frac{2\sqrt{5}}{5}$ units.

The $2\sqrt{5}$ is obtained using Pythagoras's theorem by joining each corner to the midpoint of the opposite side. Similar triangles APQ and ABE can now be used to show that the side of the small square is the same as AP, since

$\frac{AP}{AQ} = \frac{AB}{AE}$

and $AP = \frac{2}{\sqrt{5}} = \frac{2\sqrt{5}}{5}$

It is easy to see how to place the nine pieces to form five squares. (This problem is the reverse of dissecting a Greek cross (five squares) to form a square. Can you rearrange the pieces to form the cross?)

14. **Ayford: v. Beeford 2–2, v. Seaford 3–1, v. Deeford 4–3;**
Beeford: v. Seeford 1–1, v. Deeford 2–1; Seaford v. Deeford 3–2.

There were six games, so 60 points were scored for results and $(34 + 25 + 20 + 6) - 60 = 25$ points for the goals. The maximum points for a win or a draw, since a goal was scored by both sides in every game, is Ayford 25, Beeford 20, Seaford 15 and Deeford 0, so these were the actual points $(25 + 20 + 15 + 0 = 60)$. Deeford lost all three games. Beeford could not have won two games as the scores would need to be at least 2–1, 3–? and 1–?, giving 26 points.

Hence Beeford had a win (v. Deeford) and draws of 2–2 and 1–1, with the score against Deeford 2–1.

Seaford must have won with at least 3 goals, leaving their draw with Beeford 1–1, so Ayford and Beeford drew 2–2.

If Deeford scored only 1 goal against Seaford, they scored 4 against Ayford who must have scored 5 to win, leaving only 2 for their other win – already used by Beeford. Hence Seaford beat Deeford 3–2 and lost to Ayford 1–3.

Ayford thus beat Deeford 4–3.

15.

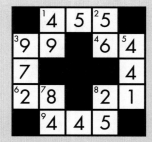

From 1-down and 3-across, 1-down ends in 4, 5 or 9; the squares of the difference between the digits of 25 and 64 are not two-digit numbers (8-down); hence 1-down is 49, 3 across is 99 and 8 down is 25.

4-across must be 27 or 64; if 27, then 5-down is 729 (27^2) or 784 (28^2), neither of which have the same final digit as 8-across; thus 4-across is 64, 5-down must be 441 and 8-across is 21, making 6-across 49 – 21 = 28.

1-across is 403, 429, 455 or 481 with digit-sums 7, 15, 14 and 13 respectively; to satisfy 2-down, therefore, 1-across is 455 and 2-down is 56 (= 4 × 14).

3-down is 972 (use the digit-sum to check multiples of 9) and 7-down is 84, so 9 across must be 445.

16. **40 unit squares in a 5 by 8 grid give a total of 100 squares.** First, note that the shorter side of the rectangle cannot be greater than 6 units, since a grid 7 by 7 gives 49 + 36 + 25 + 16 + 9 + 4 + 1 > 100 squares (counting squares 1 by 1, 2 by 2 etc.).

Obviously we could have 100 squares in a row (shorter side 1 unit); with shorter side 2 units and longer side n (>2) units, we require

$$2n + 1(n - 1) = 100$$
$$3n = 101 \text{ which has no solution.}$$

Continuing the same way with shorter side 3, 4, 5 or 6:

(3) $3n + 2(n - 1) + 1(n - 2) = 100$
   $6n = 104$ (no solution)

(4) $4n + 3(n - 1) + 2(n - 2) + 1(n - 3) = 100$
   $10n = 110$

giving n = 11, a 4-by-11 rectangle with 44 + 30 + 18 + 8 = 100 squares

(5) $5n + 4n(n - 1) + 3(n - 2) + 2(n - 3) + 1(n - 4) = 100$
   $15n = 120$

giving n = 8, a 5-by-8 rectangle, and 40 + 28 + 18 + 10 + 4 = 100 squares.

(6) $6n + 5(n - 1) + 4(n - 2) + 3(n - 3) + 2(n - 4) + 1(n - 5) = 100$
   $21n = 135$ (no solution)

Of the three possible solutions which give 100 squares in total, the smallest number of unit squares for the grid is 8 × 5 = 40.

17. **Robert: b. 1377 (MCCCLXXVII), d. 1428 (MCDXXVIII);**
    Alice: b. 1393 (MCCCXCIII), d. 1429 (MCDXXIX). Since Alice died in the year
    following Robert's own death, and there is a reduction of two numerals in the dates,
    the units digits must have gone from 8 (VIII) to 9 (IX). Robert was thus born in _ _ _ 7
    and Alice in _ _ _ 3.
    Since Alice was 35 when Robert died, she was 16 years younger than him, so the tens
    figure in her birth year is two more than that in his. Since VII and III have the same
    number of numerals, and Alice's birth year has one numeral fewer than Robert's, the
    tens have reduced by one numeral; the only possibility is LXX to XC.
    Using their ages, we now have:
    Robert: b. + + + + LXXVII,   d. + + + XXVIII;
    Alice: b. + + + + XCIII,   d. + + + XXIX.
    The only possibility for the hundreds numerals (with 0 or 1 in the thousands place) to
    shorten by 1 when increased by 1 is going from CCC to CD; since there are 4
    numerals in the earlier century there must also be an M.

18. **Rag is a fixer, Tag a Shilly-shally and Bobtail a Goodie.** (Note that the
    question allows more than one in the same tribe.)
    Rag is not a Goodie or all would be Goodies and none different as Tag and Bobtail
    stated.
    Tag is not a Fixer or Bobtail would also be a Fixer and lying which makes Rag a Fixer
    with his first statement true.
    Bobtail is not a Fixer – again, that would make them all Fixers with Rag's first statement
    true.
    Tag is not a Goodie or Rag and Bobtail would both be Shilly-shallies with Rag telling
    lies both times.
    Hence Tag is a Shilly-shally; if Tag's first statement is false, Bobtail is a Shilly-shally and
    so is Rag, making both of Rag's statements true.
    Tag's first statement must be true, and since Bobtail is not a Fixer, Bobtail is a Goodie.
    Since Bobtail's statements are both true, Rag is not a Goodie or a Shilly-shally, so Rag
    is a Fixer.
    (An alternative method is to start by noting that each contradicts both of the others;
    hence there cannot be two Goodies or two Fixers, so at least one is a Shilly-shally.)

19. One solution:

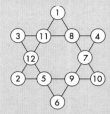

Since the sum of the first twelve natural numbers is 78 and each number appears in two rows, each row sum is $78 \times 2 \div 6 = 26$.

Since the star points also add to 26 and the other six numbers are common to both triangles, the corners of each triangle add up to 13.

The possible sets (in pairs) of three numbers whose sum is 13 are:

(a)	(1,2,10)	and	(3,4,6)
(b)	(1,3,9)	and	(2,4,7)
(c)	(1,3,9)	and	(2,5,6)
(d)	(1,4,8)	and	(2,5,6)
(e)	(1,5,7)	and	(3,4,6)
(f)	(1,5,7)	and	(2,3,8)

An exhaustive proof of all possibilities might make a profitable project; in fact there are just six essentially different solutions (from *A Puzzle Mine* by H. E. Dudeney, a collection of puzzles which first appeared in the World War I army magazine *Blighty*). The solution given above is repeated so that you can easily place the other solutions in the appropriate circles:

type (a)	1	3	11	8	4	12	7	2	5	9	10	6
type (a)	1	4	12	7	3	11	8	2	5	9	10	6
type (b)	1	4	10	5	7	12	11	3	8	6	9	2
type (d)	1	5	9	10	2	12	7	4	3	11	8	6
type (f)	1	3	9	6	8	11	12	5	10	4	7	2
type (f)	1	3	9	12	2	11	6	5	4	10	7	8

There are no solutions of type (c) or type (e).

20. One solution

Day 1: (A,B,C), (D,E,F), (G,H,I)　　**Day 2:** (A,D,G), (B,E,H), (C,F,I)
Day 3: (E,A,F), (H,D,B), (I,G,C)　　**Day 4:** (I,A,H), (F,B,G), (E,C,D)
Day 5: (A,C,H), (D,F,G), (E,I,B)　　**Day 6:** (A,G,E), (F,H,B), (C,I,D)

Each prisoner must be in the middle for two of the days and on the outside for the other four days as they must all have eight different 'companions'.

Further, no pair of prisoners can be in the middle on more than one day (try it). Even with this knowledge it is a matter of trial and error.

One efficient way is to write the letters in the form of squares for Day 1 and Day 2:

Day 1　A B C　　　　　　Day 2　A D G
　　　　D E F　　　　　　　　　　B E H
　　　　G H I　　　　　　　　　　C F I

Then alternate their columns to get the middle prisoners each day. If we then allocate A's partners as shown, we have the following pattern:

```
A B C          A D G          E A F   I A H   A C _   A G _
D E F          B E H          _ D _   _ B _   _ F _   _ H _
G H I          C F I          _ G _   _ C _   _ I _   _ I _
```

E must now partner C on Day 4, I on Day 5 and G on Day 6.

F must partner B on Day 4, H on Day 6, and D and G on Day 5.

H must partner C on Day 5, D on Day 3 and B on Day 6.

I must partner B on Day 5, C and D on Day 6, and G on Day 3.

Finally, there are two choices to complete the pattern – B or C can partner D on Day 3, with C or B to partner G; then on Day 4 G or D will partner B and D or G will partner C.

(An appropriate computer program could be used to find all essentially different solutions to this problem.)

Appendix

Problems by mathematical topic

References here are to the problems in Benders and Bogglers (the latter shown in bold type); some problems contain more than one topic.

Alphametics	1a	1d	2b	2g	3d	4b
	4e	5a	5e	6a	7e	7g
	8b	8f	9a	9h	10f	**4**
Area	2d	3a	4a	5h	7a	8h
	10e	10g				
Basic arithmetic	2a	2e	3c	7d	8g	**7**
	15					
Counting techniques	1f	2h	7f	9g	**2**	**16**
Diophantine equations (whole numbers)	6c	6g	8h	9e		
Inequalities	1c	3h	**8**			
Logic (elimination)	1g	2c	2f	3b	3g	5c
	5f	6e	7c	7h	8c	9b
	10d	**1**	**6**	**11**	**14**	
Logic (true or false)	1c	4g	5b	9f	**18**	
Proportion	1b	1e	4d	6b	**10**	**12**
Pythagoras	3a	4a	5h	7a	8d	8h
	10e	**5**	**9**	**13**		
Quadratic equations	1b	3e	8d	**12**		
Similar figures	6f	**9**				
Simple equations	1e	4f	6d	8a		
Simultaneous equations	3h	4d	6b	9c	10c	**10**

Index of titles

Index